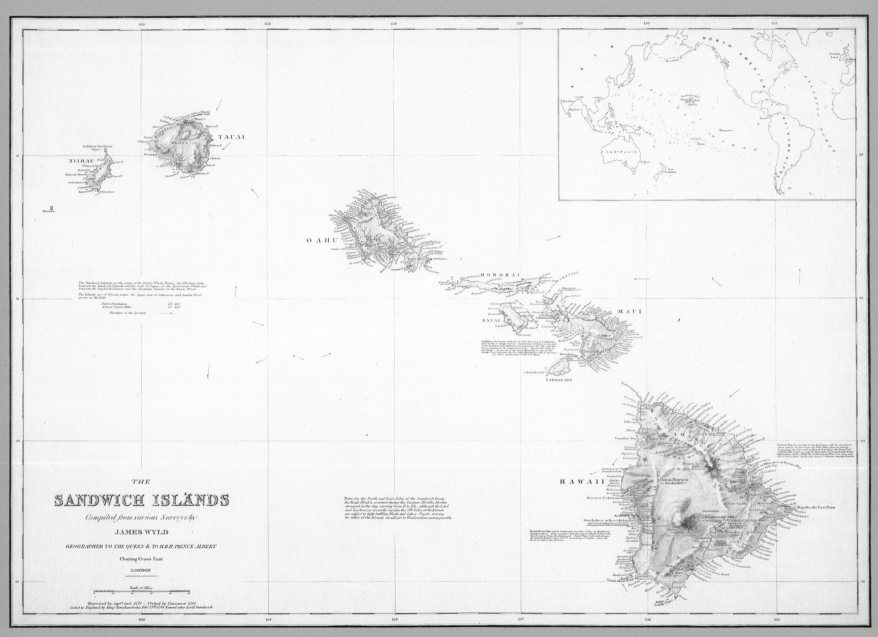

Antique map of Hawaii courtesy Library of Congress

*To the
people of Hawaii,
with affection and admiration
for the world they have
preserved and created*

Late afternoon sun highlights a young hula student practicing an ancient symbol of Hawaii's culture.

Hawaiian World, Hawaiian Heart

Text and photographs by
Roger A. LaBrucherie

Imágenes Press

*Sunset along
Kauai's Na Pali
Coast, seen from
Ke'e Beach*

Foreword

It is often remarked that there are two Hawaiis—the one visited by the tourists, and the one known to those who make Hawaii their home. For the outsider, Hawaii is all too often beaches, swaying palms, hula girls; for many who come to visit the islands, 'Hawaii' means Waikiki and its justly famous beach. Each year millions of visitors come to these islands, seeking a few days of warmth, a sunny beach, escape; for many of these millions, reared in a world of seasons, cold, city, and removed from nature, Hawaii is an exotic land, a paradise—dare I say it—a kind of Disneyland, created just for them, for their relaxation; a place without a history, without a "real" people; an artificiality.

For the *kamaaina*, as Hawaii's residents are known, the islands' physical beauty is just one part of their appeal; of equal, if not greater, importance is the spirit that pervades life in the islands. It is not a quality easy to express in a few words, although more often that not it is encapsulated as "the Aloha Spirit." I came to see it as a gentleness in the approach to life, a generosity toward others.

This is primarily a photographic book, and of course it contains many pictures of the Hawaii which visitors come to see, for Hawaii is richly endowed with scenic beauty. But Hawaii is also much more: a chain of islands with a wealth of history and culture, a multi-racial society unlike any other within the United States, or perhaps the world . . ..

On my arrival in Hawaii two years ago I was as ignorant of this history and culture as are most *malihini*, as newcomers are known. I was not sure which island Honolulu was on; I was confused by the name of 'Hawaii' the island, and 'Hawaii' the islands; I did not know that Diamond Head is a crater, rather than a mountain ridge. The months I spent traveling the islands, photographing, interviewing, and researching were a journey, a journey in which I got to know this island State as well, perhaps, as an outsider could in a reasonably short length of time. The result is what you will see here.

Hawaiian World, Hawaiian Heart is my sixth in a series of photographic-essay books on various places, all with a similar theme. I explained that theme in an earlier work about Barbados, and I will use the same thought here, for I find that I can not improve upon it now: ". . . As with my previous books, this one is an attempt to capture the essence of a place and its people, primarily for the person who has had only a relatively brief time to spend there.

". . . ever since I first lived abroad, well over a decade ago, I have been aware of the particular perspective and fresh insight a foreigner's eye can provide in looking at a country. Like a child, a newcomer is blessed with the ignorance that can lead to curiosity; from curiosity, to investigation; and from investigation, to understanding. It is that somewhat childlike curiosity, illuminated by understanding, that I have always tried to bring to my portrayal of a country, and in that respect this book has much in common with its predecessors . . ..

"It must be recognized that that special perspective does not come bias-free: an outsider necessarily carries with him a set of values shaped by his own culture. Even were it remotely possible, I would not attempt to define all those values, but I feel I should comment on one: coming as I do from a place where much is new, big, and impersonal, I am greatly captivated by those aspects of a country which are traditional, small and personal."

Thus, the reader should not be surprised to see a considerable emphasis in this book on the people, culture, and history of Hawaii. While such a bias necessarily means slighting certain other aspects (there are relatively few photographs of Hawaii's beaches, for example), I hope that this deficiency will be understood and accepted—especially in view of the ample coverage given those aspects by already-existing books about the islands.

As I have said, I came to Hawaii with a great deal of ignorance about the islands—sharing, perhaps, the limited perception about the State common to many new arrivals. In the course of my journey through Hawaii I began to grasp the fullness and complexity of its history and culture; it is my hope that this book will impart to the visitor a glimmer of that "other" Hawaii, and that it may lead him to further exploration and understanding of the Hawaiians' world.

Symbol of the tropics: the bird of paradise.

Contents

Of Pele and Polynesians: a World Emerges

In a scene as old as Hawaii itself, Pele spews from Pu'u O'o on the Big Island.

First vegetation to appear on a lava flow, a tiny fern struggles through a crack in pahoehoe lava in Hawaii Volcanoes National Park on the Big Island (this page). *Just north of Niihau, the crater shape of tiny Lehua* (opposite) *reveals the volcanic origin of the entire Hawaiian chain.*

The helicopter shudders and sways as the pilot brings us to a hover some 80 feet above the lava pond in the fading light. Photographers strain for a vantage point at the open hatch as heat floods into the cabin from the glowing, flowing mass below.

Creation, I think to myself. This is how the world formed. This is how Hawaii formed. Six hundred thousand cubic yards of lava have been flowing from this vent every day, over the hillside and through a system of underground lava tubes, for months on end. And yet, my predominant reaction, aside from my awe at seeing this primordial scene for the first time, is astonishment at how small this pond is, on the landscape below. How much land, how much island, is formed in a day? It seems miniscule against the Big Island's bulk, stretching in every direction to the horizon.

It is time, of course, which is unseen, unfathomable, incomprehensible . . .. Time beyond all our experience—for millions of years this scene has repeated itself, this outpouring from a "hot spot" deep beneath the earth's mantle, as the Pacific Mid-Ocean Plate grinds slowly, imperceptibly toward the northwest. And as that plate has passed, here and there over a distance of some fifteen hundred miles the hot spot has found weaknesses, and its molten mass has risen, bubbling, churning, flowing to the surface. Far to the northwest the record remains, in tiny islands, atolls, reefs, and submerged peaks. At the southeastern end of that chain, the newest end— at most six million years old, much of it, the Big Island included, considerably younger (meager compared to the hundreds of millions of years of the continents)— those islands are still in their glory, rising magnificently from the ocean depths, in some cases to spectacular heights, for islands so small. In the midst of the vast Pacific, over two thousand miles from the nearest continental land, five hundred from

Over uncounted millennia, time, wind and water have shaped the islands into dramatic forms: Kauai's famed Na Pali coast (opposite), and the Hamakua coastline of Hawaii, the "Big Island" (this page).

Islands of beauty and variety: a winter storm covers the summit of the Big Island's Mauna Kea ("White Mountain") in a blanket of snow (this page). The windward slopes of the islands receive heavy rainfall carried by the northeast tradewinds, and, like the Hana region of Maui, are home to uncounted, unnamed waterfalls (opposite).

More than two thousand miles from the nearest continental land, Hawaii provided ecological isolation for the occasional non-migratory birds that reached the islands, and dozens of unique species evolved. Some, like the mamo (Drepanis pacifica, this page) *proved unable to withstand the hunting and habitat loss which followed man's arrival, and are now extinct. Others, such as the Hawaiian Stilt, or Ae'o* (Himantopus mexicanus knudseni, opposite), *although endangered, have managed to survive, in part due to the establishment of wildlife preserves in various parts of the islands. [Mamo print: collection of Don Severson, Honolulu]*

the nearest island group, the islands stand isolated as are few places in the world.

Only the currents of wind and sea gave contact with the outside, and for untold centuries these forces acted on the islands. Attacking from all sides, the sea cut and gouged out bays, inlets and headlands indiscriminately. The wind was more predictable, for in these latitudes the trade winds from the northeast are a near-constant feature, and brought the rain, sometimes in torrents, to the windward slopes. Fantastic forms were eroded, mostly to windward, but in some areas through the arid lands to leeward, in the "rain shadow" of a high mountain. Being the oldest, Kauai, northwesternmost of the main islands, is the supreme example, but all the other high-rising islands—Molokai especially—display similar, if less spectacular, effects of water and time.

In the vastness of time, the wind and sea currents, with the help of birds, brought the seeds of grasses, bushes and trees which took root in the developing soil, and in turn helped to build that soil. But the lushness that one experiences in the Hawaii of today is deceptive, for the vast bulk of the plant life (including all of the flowering plants) seen in the accessible parts of the islands were introduced by man. Except for birds (and a species of bat, the only land-dwelling mammal native to Hawaii), animals had a much harder time of it: insects came on the winds, and of course fish and other sea-living creatures colonized the islands' waters and shorelines as suitable habitat developed. Considering the enormity of the distance involved, it is not surprising that other land-dwelling species are very few indeed: an extraordinary diversity of land snails (numbering over 1000 species, and of great interest to biologists for their contribution to the understanding of evolution), and several species of lizards, or more properly, geckos, which have become a popular symbol, or mascot, of the islands.

Thus for millennia the islands were formed: erupting, eroding, subsiding, reforming, and—surrounded by the vast ocean—evolving plants and animals from the lucky few which had survived the great journey into species in their vast majority unique to this island world. And always, always, there was the sea, now pounding, now peaceful, shaping and sheltering these islands, insulating them from

Hawaii offered a lush tropical para-dise, but the surrounding ocean was an all-but-insurmountable barrier to ground-dwelling species. One of the handful that survived that incredible journey was the gecko, a type of lizard (opposite, shown approxi-mately life size). Few scenes capture that lushness better than a much-photographed stream in the Big Island's Akaka Falls State Park (this page).

Two moods of the sea and shore: a late-afternoon aerial view of the Big Island's Puna coast (this page); and evening calm over an inlet near Maui's Makena Point (Kahoolawe and tiny Molokini accent the horizon, opposite).

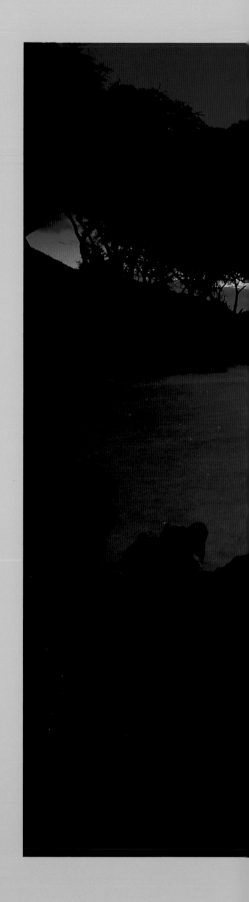

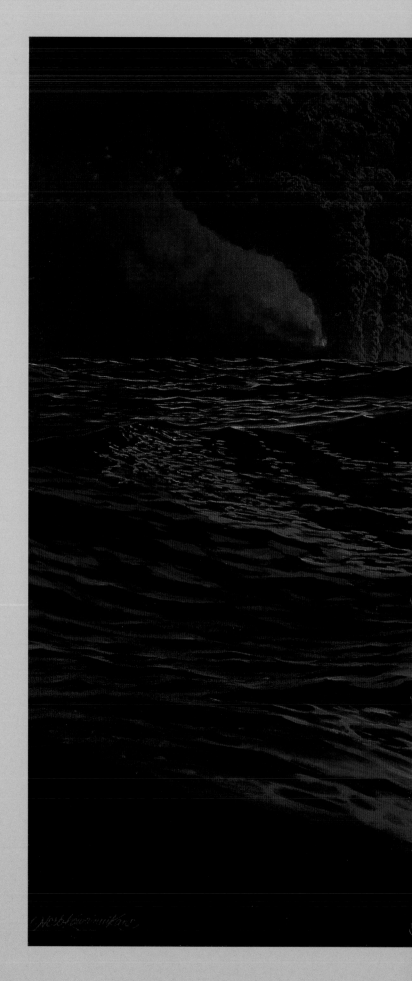

Archaeological evidence suggests that Polynesians from the Marquesas Islands, navigating huge 70-foot double-hulled canoes, were the first to settle Hawaii, perhaps as early as 500 A.D.; centuries later a new migratory wave arrived from Tahiti, soon establishing a domination over the existing population. ["Hawaii Discovery" painting, Copyright Herb Kawainui Kane: collection of the Hawaii State Foundation on Culture and the Arts]

the outside world. And the islands waited.

The surrounding ocean was vast, but it was not empty; far to the south, other islands and island groups abounded, and for centuries stretching back to near the time of Christ peoples from southeastern Asia and its neighboring islands had been spreading across the southern ocean, island-hopping in large double-hulled canoes powered by sails and paddles.

For these peoples the ocean was not a forbidding barrier, as was often the case with continental cultures. The sea was an integral part of their world, as vital as the tiny bits of land on which they lived. For the people of the southern Pacific the idea that there were other lands out of sight over the horizon was hardly revolutionary; it was simply taken for granted. Very likely the question of the world's roundness or flatness never occurred to them; almost certainly they had no fear of falling off the edge if they sailed too far . . ..

Understood in this light, the question of why then, sometime before the Ninth Century A.D. (and perhaps considerably earlier), voyagers from the Marquesas Islands set out upon the sea and discovered the Hawaiian Islands becomes less pressing; ocean voyaging was second nature to these peoples. Almost certainly we will never know their precise motivation for venturing so far, although various possibilities suggest themselves: the demand for more land due to population pressure, warfare between groups, general exploration. Certainly, given the Polynesians' skill at sailing and navigation, a chance discovery by being blown off course in a storm is unlikely in the extreme. And what is further clear from the archaeological evidence is that, once discovered,

Though lacking a writing system, pre-historic Hawaiians left an enduring, if cryptic, record in petroglyph fields throughout the islands. The most extensive of all is at Pu'u Loa, on Hawaii (opposite). Remains of settlements have been found in nearly all parts of the islands, including deep hanging valleys today considered inaccessible.

Ideal living conditions were found in the broad-bottomed river valleys on the windward sides of the islands, where an ample water supply irrigated the taro patches central to the Hawaiian diet. In Kauai's Wailua River Valley a typical village of thatched huts has been re-created at Kamokila (this page).

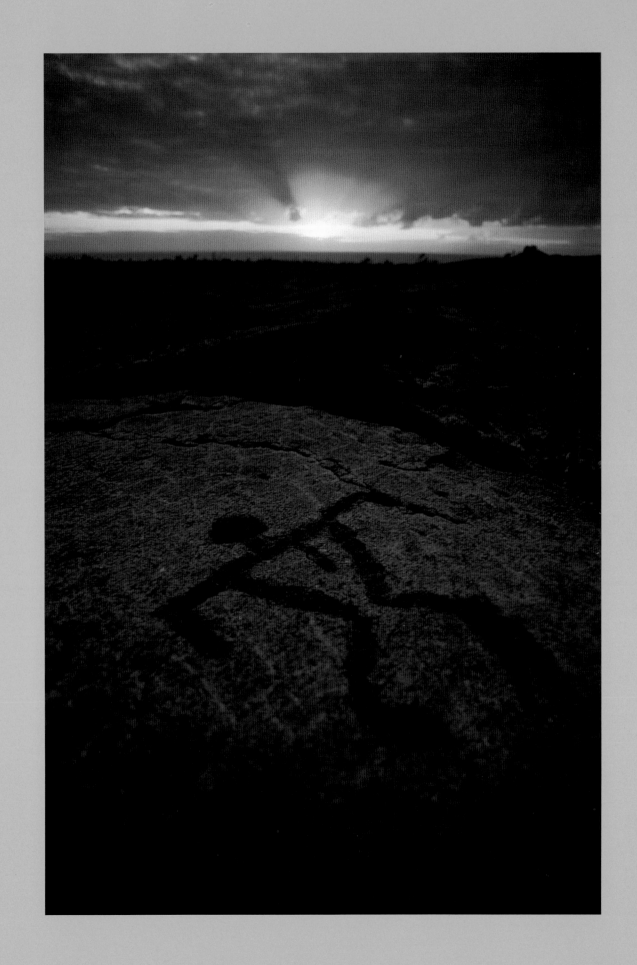

repeated voyages between Hawaii and the "home islands" were made.

The first discoverers of the islands found them empty of any significant food sources, save the fishes in the surrounding seas and birds they might catch (among them the Hawaiian goose, or *nene*, today the State bird) and thus the foods which were the staples of the ancient Hawaiian diet were those the southern colonizers brought with them: breadfruit, sweet potato, yam, coconut, banana, sugar cane, dog, pig, and of course, taro, which, when cooked, mashed and mixed with water became the mainstay of their diet, poi. The broad, flat, well-watered valleys found primarily on the islands' windward coasts, such as Wailua and Hanalei on Kauai, Halawa on Molokai, and Waipio and Waimanu on Hawaii are ideally suited to taro cultivation, and it is likely that these were the first places settled. But as the population of the islands grew and the economies of the islands developed to make trading possible, all but the most inhospitably arid areas were settled; indeed the drier western areas were often favored by the ruling classes, for whom taro cultivation was not a direct concern. Details of the early Hawaiians' culture are sketchy at best, but it is reasonable to assume that, besides food sources, they brought with them as well the elements of the culture from which they came— certainly the similarities between the cultures of the southern Pacific region and that of Hawaii at the time of Western contact were evident even to the layman, as the Europeans' journals make clear.

Whatever the traits of the earliest culture, they were eventually modified by a second wave of migration, this one from Tahiti, which occurred near the end of the Twelfth Century. The new arrivals soon dominated the resident population, occupying the top ranks of a hierarchical, feudal society in which the chiefly class, the *ali'i*, held all temporal power over the mass of the people, a power limited only by the *kahuna*, or priestly class, who interceded with and interpreted the signs of the many gods overseeing all aspects of Hawaiian life.

Although the islands were mere specks in a vast ocean, their dominant physical fact was their separation from each other by considerable ocean channels—and the result was that each island was a separate fiefdom under the independent rule of an island chief, or king.

All the land of each island, together with its adjoining coastal waters, was the property of the king (on the island of Hawaii, much larger than any of the other islands in the chain, there were at times regional chiefs, as opposed to a single king; conversely, the smaller islands, such as Lanai and Niihau were typically under the control of the chief of the large adjacent island). The king would parcel out portions in the shape of wedges—called *ahupua'a*—stretching from mountain tops to the coastal waters, to lesser alii loyal to him; they in turn would assign parcels, or *kuleana*, to commoners who had the use of the land in exchange for the payment of taxes. As in other feudal systems, land and physical protection were provided in exchange for labor (in the form of a share of the crop or other labor) and loyalty to those above.

Ancient Hawaii was a place in which protection by an overlord was vital, for despite the image widely held today of early Hawaii as a Polynesian paradise, Hawaii could be a very violent place; war between competing factions, within or between islands, especially upon the death of a ruling chief, was a constant threat, and the cost of defeat was usually death or enslavement.

Worlds Collide: of Kings, Captain Cook and Congregationalists

Ancient Hawaii was governed by a panoply of deities representing every object and force of nature, and in turn personified in idols, usually carved of wood. The small image (shown opposite), sometimes called a "house god" was very likely the personal icon of an alii or kahuna, and used in private worship. Public religious ceremonies, sometimes involving human sacrifice, were conducted by the kahuna (priests) at a multitude of heiau, or temples, (this page). Violation of a commandment, or kapu, could mean instantaneous death. [Artifact height about 14" overall: courtesy Watters O. Martin, Jr., Honolulu; heiau print by Louis Choris, 1818: collection of Don Severson, Honolulu]

The alii held life-and-death power over the commoners, and lived a life of privileged ease; but their power was not without limits. For Hawaiian society was governed by a system of *kapu* (the corresponding word would later be written *tabou* by French linguists developing a written language for French Polynesia) which embodied the dictates of the gods, as interpreted by the *kahuna*, or priests. Although there were just four principal deities, Kane, Ku, Lono, and Kanaloa (the gods of sunlight and nature; war; the sky, agriculture, and thunder; and the sea, respectively), countless other minor gods represented or controlled every conceivable object and activity. Religious ceremonies (frequently involving animal, or less commonly, human, sacrifice) were conducted at temples, or *heiau*—stone enclosures or raised platforms, containing large carved wooden statues representing the deities, and featuring wooden oracle towers. The remains of *heiau* can be seen throughout the islands to this day. Not surprisingly, the gods' will bore most heavily on commoners, but the alii class too—and especially its women—were subject to kapu as well, and the penalty for serious violation could be immediate and painful death.

By the late 18th Century, then, Hawaii had been home to an evolving culture for a thousand years or more; and with the cessation of the long-distance canoe voyages to the southern islands shortly after the Tahitian migration, the memory of, much less awareness or understanding of, any outside world had faded into the recesses of time, dimly and vaguely remembered in the *mele*, or chanted poems, which, in a culture without writing, were the present's only link with what had gone before. The isolation which had created a near-unique world of flora and fauna, had now, in a far shorter span of time, helped create a unique human culture as well, secure in its certitude. And if the gods and their kapu were severe, they also provided the confidence that life was predictable as long as kapu was observed. But as with many things which grow up in the security of isolation, Hawaii was soon to discover how fragile that security can be.

So for a thousand years or more, the peoples of the islands had lived with the vicissitudes of nature, the gods and man: for a thousand cycles of the sun's yearly swing the Hawaiians had learned to live with tsunami, torrential rain, Pele's recurrent eruptions on the islands of Hawaii and Maui, warfare, and the precarious severity of the kapu system. The islands were paradise for the alii, an arduous existence for

the commoners, virtual enslavement for an unlucky few. But for all that, it was a stable world where man had come to terms with nature—and it was a generous nature: blessed by one of the most equable climates in the world, bounded by warm seas, life was taken at a generous pace—time enough for hula, for making and giving leis, for sporting contests, for swimming and "wave sliding" on koa-wood boards. Despite isolation from their founding culture, the Hawaiians had developed the arts of featherwork and kapa-making to levels unsurpassed anywhere in Polynesia. And though the islands were not richly endowed with fertile soil, the Hawaiian diet was a simple one, consisting largely of fish and poi; and by the mid-Eighteenth Century the islands were supporting a population estimated at well over 200,000 people.

Then on January 18, 1778, by the calendar of the Western world, a day which began like the uncounted others which stretched seamlessly back in time, the isolation of that world was shattered forever. A sharp-eyed lookout on the Waianae coast of Oahu may have been the first to see them—but at the great distance he may have thought he had imagined them, the two tiny specks of white, moving steadily to the north. The following day the natives of Kauai knew that the white sails and the two "floating islands" which bore them were no apparition, and as Captain James Cook's *Discovery* and *Resolution* neared Kauai's southern shore, they set out in their outriggers to challenge or welcome, as circumstances might dictate, these world-shaking newcomers.

Charged by the government of King George III to reconnoiter the Pacific and to find a northern passage around the American continent, Cook's mission was one of exploration, not conquest. Repeated contacts with Polynesians of the southern Pacific during two previous expeditions had taught him that the natives of these islands were welcoming if dealt with in a friendly manner, and so it proved in this case, for upon seeing that these strange men in their enormous ships had no aggressive intent, the paddlers threw their poised stones overboard, and made signs of welcome.

In search of safe anchorage, the vessels coasted the southern shore toward the west, trailed by awe-struck natives offering gifts of food. On the following day, the 20th of January, the ships hove to off the village of Waimea, where a good-sized river entered the sea. Several days were spent visiting the area, replenishing food and water supplies. Then, after two weeks of friendly exchange (including an overnight stay by a stranded boat party on neighboring Niihau, which introduced venereal disease to the islands, the first of many western diseases which would eventually decimate the vulnerable Hawaiian population), Cook and his crew sailed off toward the north, in search of the northern passage, leaving the people of the Sandwich Islands (for so he had named them, in honor of the first Lord of the Admiralty) to wonder at what had just transpired.

What to think? Gods or men? Demigods? Whatever their thoughts, the news of the encounter spread quickly throughout the islands; and when, in January of 1779, the *Resolution* and *Discovery* arrived at Kealakekua Bay on the west coast of the island of Hawaii, returned from a year in Arctic waters in fruitless searching for the northern passage, the Hawaiians had decided: Cook was the god Lono, and he and his men would be honored accordingly.

Cook and his crew, of course, were unaware of his changed status, and continued dealing with the natives as they had done before, trading bits of iron—a substance new to Hawaii but quickly appreciated for its potential—for water, food and sexual favors from the willing women. Indeed, iron was so highly prized that the Hawaiians did not hesitate to take what they might lay their hands on, when opportunities arose, for the Hawaiians recognized iron for what it was: a revolutionary material which could ensure victory in warfare. But for the British this opportunism was not only theft, it was potentially disastrous to an expedition dependent on its own resources and thousands of miles from home; transgressors, if caught, were dealt with summarily. Concurrently, the Hawaiians were doubtless beginning to have further thoughts about the status of these white creatures, who, language, clothing, and other possessions aside, were, after all, very much like themselves: what manner of god would have the same physical needs as their own, and besides, barter for them?

The ships remained for nearly three weeks, with numerous incidents and misunderstandings transpiring—many of which threw the Europeans' god-status further into doubt—before again departing for the north. But a sudden squall and a broken mast forced their return to Kealakekua Bay for repairs, and within a few days tensions had risen over another series of incidents involving theft of property. Then the Discovery's cutter was stolen, and Cook himself went ashore with a small armed force to obtain its return. Cook's plan was to take Kalaniopuu, chief of the island, hostage to gain return of the cutter. When the Hawaiians sensed his purpose, they rushed forward to defend their king; a warrior struck a blow, Cook fell; another thrust his dagger home. In the flash of violence four marines of the guard party and several Hawaiians were also killed. The ships remained a few more days, with better relations eventually restored, but not before the Hawaiians had experienced the bloody power of Western weaponry. Then the ships set sail, visiting Oahu and Kauai before departing for the north and the resumption of the expedition.

Thus Captain Cook, a legend in his lifetime, surely England's—and perhaps the world's—greatest navigator, died in the land, and at the hands of the people, he introduced to the world. The Hawaiians could not know of his stature in the world outside; but they now knew a fact of far greater import: there *was* another world beyond the horizon, and it had powers far beyond the ability of the alii and *kapu* to control.

It was several years before the outside world intruded again, but as news of Cook's discovery spread, it was only a matter of time before other ships would call at the islands: for their remote location in the central Pacific, which had for so long kept the islands isolated, now made them singularly attractive as a haven for ships plying the mid-Pacific.

Toward the end of the Eighteenth Century fur traders were plying the coastline of America from California northward, and soon they as well as trans-Pacific merchantmen began calling at the islands for respite from the northern cold, replenishment of supplies, or simply relief from the tedium of long months at sea—for the Hawaiians, and especially their women, were gaining a reputation for welcoming hospitality.

For the Hawaiians, too, these visits were welcome: for in exchange for food, water, and the bodies of their women—all readily available at the islands—they gained access to all manner of new and exciting Western goods. And no Western novelty was more sought after than firearms, for the Hawaiians had been introduced to their deadly power as early as Captain Cook's first visit, and the lesson had not been lost on them.

No one saw the revolutionary potential of firearms and other European technology better than a young and physically powerful warrior chief on the island of Hawaii named Kamehameha, who by 1780 had become the overlord of the Kohala district. Present at Kealakekua Bay during Cook's visit, Kamehameha

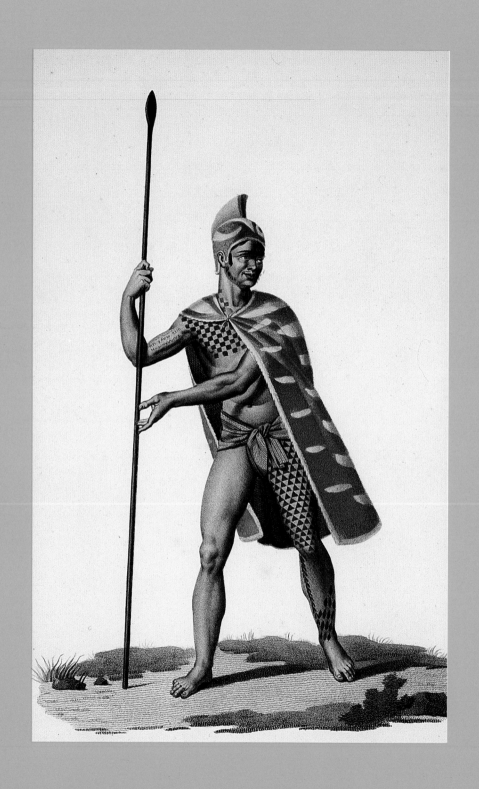

Although the Hawaiians had a fierce warrior tradition, English Captain James Cook's discovery of the islands in January, 1778 met a friendly reception. On his return a year later, however, Cook was killed in a shoreline skirmish at Kealakekua Bay on the island of Hawaii when an altercation over a stolen cutter suddenly flared into fatal violence. [Warrior print by Jacques Arago, 1819: collection of Don Severson, Honolulu; "The Death of Captain Cook" by John Webber, ca. 1780: museum collection, Hawaiian Islands (anonymous by request)]

After centuries as separate chiefdoms, the islands were for the first time united in 1795 when Kamehameha, overlord of Hawaii Island, conquered Maui, Lanai and Molokai, then crossed the Kaiwi Channel and defeated the defenders of Oahu at the Battle of Nuuanu Pali. After two failed attempts at invasion, Kauai would be added to the kingdom by treaty in 1810. [Portrait of Kamehameha, artist unknown, ca. 1815: collection of the Bishop Museum, Honolulu; "Battle of the Nuuanu Pali" painting copyright Herb Kawainui Kane: collection of Nick G. Maggos, courtesy of Kamehameha Schools]

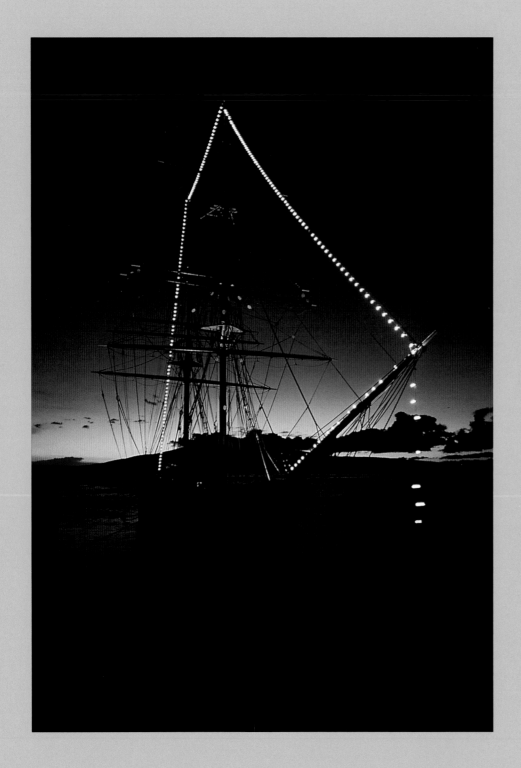

In the years following Cook's discovery, Hawaii increasingly became a rest and trading point for explorers and traders. The Cartha-ginian, a replica of a 19th-Century square-rigger moored at Lahaina, Maui, is a reminder of those early European and American contacts (this page). *Exposure to Western ideas slowly eroded the foundation of the islands' traditional religion, and in 1819 Kamehameha II, son and successor to Kamehameha the Great, formally overthrew the kapu system. Later that year a visiting French vessel,* L'Uranie (opposite), *was the setting for the baptism of Kalanimoku, a high chief of the kingdom.* [Baptism print by Crepin, after Arago, 1819: collection of Don Severson, Honolulu]

In quick succession two outside influences were introduced into the kingdom which would profoundly affect its future. In 1819 the first whaling ship visited the islands; over the ensuing decades Lahaina and Honolulu would become the favored rest and refitting stations for hundreds of ships of the Pacific whaling fleet. The following year the first company of Protestant missionaries reached Hawaii after a six-month voyage around Cape Horn from New England. In a re-creation of the missionary era staged weekly at Honolulu's Mission Houses Museum, Laurel Spencer portrays Jerusha Chamberlain of that Pioneer Company (this page). [Whaling aquatint by C. Hulsart, 1833: collection of the New Bedford Whaling Museum]

had spent time aboard the British ships, and had had ample opportunity to absorb at length and firsthand the significance of European weapons and skills. Though portraits of him from later in life tend to show a kindly or statesmanlike mien, contemporary accounts and the facts of his life leave no doubt that Kamehameha had courage, ruthlessness, guile, and ambition, as well as political vision and a sharp intelligence, in abundance. When Kalaniopuu, chief of the island of Hawaii and uncle to Kamehameha, died in 1782, leaving a divided political inheritance, Kamehameha moved boldly and swiftly against his cousin, Kiwalao, Kalaniopuu's son and designated successor, to assert his pretensions to sole control of the island. Forming strategic alliances with other regional chiefs, Kamehameha emerged victorious from a series of battles, in which he steadily perfected the use of European weapons and advisors, and by 1782 had gained control of the northern and western regions of the island of Hawaii.

As has been mentioned, the islands had historically been separate kingdoms, with no ruler able to assert control over the whole; for an attacker with designs on another island had not only to overcome a hazardous ocean channel: he was going to be met by a roughly equal force once he landed. Historically these odds had been only rarely overcome; no more than two or three islands had come under the tenuous hold of a single chief. Kamehameha's genius lay in recognizing that European weaponry, transport, and advisors (or mercenaries), if marshaled quickly, presented the opportunity to upset the old balance. Kamehameha did just that.

In 1790 he moved against Maui, and in a bloody battle in the Iao Valley, routed the defending forces. Then unsettled conditions back on Hawaii forced him to abandon his Maui gains and return to the Big Island to consolidate his home position. Five years passed, and he saw his chance again: gathering his fleet of war canoes, he quickly reconquered Maui and Molokai, then crossed the Kaiwi Channel and landed his war canoes on Waikiki and nearby beaches and pursued the defenders up the Nuuanu Valley to the precipitous pali, where those who were not slain were forced over the cliff to their death. Now Maui, Molokai, Lanai and Oahu were under Kamehameha's dominion, and would henceforth be part of his kingdom, the kingdom of *Hawai'i*.

Only Kauai (and its dependency, Niihau) remained to be conquered, and Kamehameha immediately began planning their invasion; twice in the next ten years invading forces were readied, and twice *force majeure* stopped them before crossing the channel. Perhaps sensing the gods were not with him, Kamehameha lay aside his dream of total unification, and spent the remaining years of his life consolidating his kingdom, enriching the royal treasury, ensuring his dynasty, and enjoying the fruits of victory. (Defended by the unpredictable 90-mile Kauai channel, Kauai never fell to invasion, and was incorporated into Kamehameha's kingdom in 1810 only by treaty, under which Kauai's King Kaumualii acknowledged Kamehameha's suzerainty over him.)

The occasional visits of foreign ships continued, and the islands began acquiring other aspects of Western culture besides the weapons and goods which had attracted the Hawaiians from the beginning: the occasional seaman, seeing that a life in the islands with a native wife could be a better prospect than growing old on the seas, jumped ship. The port towns, especially Lahaina and Honolulu, began acquiring a small resident population of foreigners—and not necessarily the best products of Western society, either: the inevitable drifter and n'ere-do-well showed up, as well as the petty merchant, and soon the port towns were sprouting grog shops and small provision houses. With each such addition the ports became more attractive to passing ships, and visits became more frequent. Then in the early 1800s the visits of trading ships became all the more frequent when sandalwood trees, highly valued in China for their fragrant wood, first attracted commercial interest. With a free valuable trading resource at hand and a zeal for acquiring Western ships, weapons and goods, within a few years Kamehameha had stripped the mountainsides of sandalwood, sending the commoners into the forests in search of the trees, and in the process wreaking havoc on taro cultivation, creating widespread hunger.

As Hawaii's existence became better known, the great powers with interests in the Pacific—England, France, Spain, and Russia—took note of the islands, and sent the occasional ship or agent to investigate. None, however, saw at that point a colonial prize worth the effort: the islands were tiny, without significant resources, under the control of a powerful local king who welcomed all friendly visitors, and all the great powers had interests elsewhere too important to be compromised by an unprofitable distraction. In fact, an independent, neutral kingdom at the islands suited them all, providing a safe haven in mid-Pacific at no cost.

As the first two decades of the 19th Century unrolled, Hawaiians increasingly discovered that foreign ships were bringing more than Western goods and men: the venereal disease that arrived with Cook's first visit has already been mentioned; in 1804 a severe epidemic, very likely cholera or typhoid fever, wiped out thousands of the islanders. Polynesian origins and centuries of isolation meant the population had no natural immunity to European diseases; measles, influenza, and other lesser afflictions often proved fatal. Of perhaps greater long-term consequence to Hawaiian culture were equally invisible accouterments of the Westerners: their ideas and values. It was apparent, once the initial shock at their very existence had worn off, that these men lived by a set of rules very different from the system of kapu which made the alii and kahuna all-powerful in Hawaiian society.

Even more, as Westerners went about their way, it became obvious that they violated, often as not in complete ignorance, kapu prohibitions such as those against eating with women or touching a chief, with impunity. And as Hawaiians came to understand, however imperfectly, that these outsiders were men, rather than gods, just like themselves, they had to begin doubting the power and authority of the alii and kahuna, the power of the gods behind *kapu*, and, indeed, the unthinkable, the very existence of the gods themselves.

It was not the gods and kapu alone which were brought into question. For while the white men, too, had superiors and inferiors, such as the captain and officers of a ship, it was clear that the relationship of "commoner" to "chief" among Westerners was very different from that the Hawaiians knew. Fundamental to the difference, though unstated, was the concept that no human being, whether chief or commoner, was subject to the whim or arbitrary power of another. This of course was a revolutionary concept in Hawaii, where commoners were utterly at the mercy of alii and kahuna.

While Kamehameha lived no one dared openly challenge the kapu system, although kapus were being surreptitiously broken. Upon Kamehameha's death in 1819, his favorite wife, Kaahumanu, seized the opportunity presented by the weakness of Kamehameha's son and successor, Liholiho (Kamehameha II), to bring about the downfall of the kapu system, and to strengthen her own position within the ruling elite at the same time.

As has been mentioned, the kapu system was especially oppressive to women, and had doubtless been evolved to keep both women and commoners in subjugation. The arrival of Westerners was particularly subversive to the system's domination of women, for the early Western arrivals were all men, woman-hungry from long deprivation, and used to the idea of women as sexually modest and chaste. Their attitudes had subtly enhanced women's status in Hawaiian society, and the traditional order—as codified by the kapu system—was out of step with this new perception. Thus when Kaahumanu persuaded Liholiho to publicly transgress—and therefore effectively abolish—the kapu system by sitting down to eat with women, the groundwork had been prepared for years. Kapu died without a struggle.

So in 1819 Hawaiian society was a rudderless ship upon the sea: its religious and moral underpinnings asunder, under constant bombardment from Westerners' ideas and demands, and, at the helm, after 25 years under the great unifier, Kamehameha I, his weak-willed, fun-loving son, Liholiho. Onto that sea were about to burst two powerful influences, both pulling Hawaiian society toward the west—in two conflicting directions.

The first influence was that of the whalers, flying flags of various nations, but principally out of New England; by the early 1800s the Atlantic whaling grounds were beginning to show signs of depletion, and the whaling ships had rounded Cape Horn in search of better pickings. In 1819 the first whale ship visited Hawaii, about the same time the sperm whale grounds off Japan were discovered, and from that point the number of whaling ships in the Pacific grew steadily. And the whalemen found that in Hawaii they had ports for rest, recreation and refurbishing as perfect as they could have asked for: near to the whaling grounds, but with warm water, sun, and women, and a relaxed moral attitude in which to enjoy them. Within a few years their favorite ports of Lahaina and Honolulu were booming with rooming houses and grog shops, the streets full of carousing, brawling tars washing the salt from their throats. The whalemen had found their paradise—what could dampen the party?

Ironically, just about the time the first whaling ships were calling in Hawaiian waters, the answer was embarking for Hawaii in Boston harbor, and, in further irony, the Protestant missionaries setting out in that October of 1819 were products of the same hardy New England soil from which the whalemen had

Between 1820 and 1848 some 150 Protestant missionaries would be sent out to the islands, establishing "stations" throughout the kingdom. Their central purpose was to bring the gospel to the Hawaiian people; to do so they created a writing system for the Hawaiian language, taught the bulk of the population to read, and translated the Bible into Hawaiian. At the Mission Houses Museum in central Honolulu (this page), the original notebooks of those missionary translations are still preserved (opposite).

In the 1820s and 30s the presence and influence of Westerners and their ideas would gather steam. The alii were the missionaries' earliest and most influential adherents, and their conversion to Christianity ensured its rapid spread throughout the population. (The print this page depicts Kinau, regent and primary counselor to Kamehameha III, returning from Sunday services at Honolulu's Kawaiahao Church.) For centuries the Hawaiians had cultivated their taro patches, much like farmers on Maui's Keanae Peninsula (opposite) do today; but large areas of the islands had never known cultivation, and in the 1830s some among the growing foreign population saw the potential for great profit if the right crop could be found for those lands. [Kinau print by Masselot, 1837: collection of Don Severson, Honolulu]

sprung.

When Western ships first reached Hawaii, Hawaiians had been as fascinated by what they promised of the outside world as the explorers were by what they encountered in the islands; as early as the 1780s Hawaiian youth (the first of what would become a long line of merchant seamen) had "shipped out" on passing vessels, and by 1819 a small group of these adventurous young men had reached New England, home base for most of the American merchant vessels of the era. Through these young men the New England Protestant community—predominantly Presbyterian and Congregationalist denominations—learned of conditions in the Sandwich Islands, and resolved to send a "company" of American missionaries to the islands to convert the islanders to Christianity.

On October 23, 1819 the "Pioneer Company" of twenty-two people—seven missionary couples, five children, and three Hawaiian "helpers"—boarded the brig *Thaddeus* for the six month voyage around Cape Horn, arriving off the coast of the island of Hawaii on March 30, 1820. Their first task was to secure royal permission to settle in the islands and pursue the conversion of the Hawaiian people. They presented themselves to Liholiho, but the king was unsure. "Come back tomorrow," they were told. For days the king vacillated, torn by conflicting counsel. Would they be sent packing, never to even have the chance of preaching the Lord's Word? No one surveying the scene would have dreamt that these mild-mannered, soberly-attired men, women and children in tow, bedraggled and haggard from six seasick-wracked months around the Horn on the pitiable *Thaddeus*, presented an historic moment for Hawaii. Surely no one paid more than passing heed to the tiny band of supplicants pressing their case before the king and his advisors. But in the balance hung the future of a kingdom.

Finally Liholiho decided: "All right—a year. Then we'll see." It was not the most auspicious of beginnings, but it would have to do. And now came the hardest part of all—united by the past six months of adversity and the *Thaddeus'* cramped quarters, the group had to split up, divide its forces to reach the greatest number of possible converts. Some would remain there on the Big Island at Kailua, while the rest would go to Waimea on Kauai, and to Honolulu. Their grand work could begin.

The missionaries had come to Hawaii to preach the way of Christ, to convert the heathen. But not for these sturdy Calvinists an easy, ship-board baptism; not for them a mere ceremonial "acceptance" of Christianity. No, for a true conversion a full, informed *understanding* of the Scriptures was required. And doctrine and practicality insisted that the potential convert be able to independently read and judge for himself the words of the Bible. But the Hawaiians had no written language; only a few thoroughly understood English, and no more than a handful had a command of written English. So a writing system for Hawaiian was needed, and once that was created, the Hawaiians would have to be taught to read it. It was a daunting task, but the missionaries were prepared for it. Among their number were scholars who could refer to Greek and Hebrew texts for Biblical translation; another was a printer by trade, and among the items carried from Boston was Hawaii's first printing press.

Before they could write Hawaiian, however, they would have to learn to speak it—for like many a language student, they had learned that the Hawaiian they painstakingly learned from their Hawaiian helpers back in New England and on board the *Thaddeus* bore scant relation to the rapid-fire normal speech of the natives. They persevered, and slowly acquired a proficiency. Now for the writing. But in comparing notes, the company discovered the problem which had been perplexing new arrivals since Cook's time: it was difficult, if not impossible, to decide exactly what sounds they were hearing. One time it sounded like "Honolulu," another, more like "Hanaruru"; moreover, there were regional differences: on Kauai (which early explorers had heard and written as "Atooi"), a "t" was heard in words where other islanders pronounced something closer to a "k." But a choice had to be made. After discussion, the group decided on an alphabet of 17 letters, and in January of 1822, struck off 500 copies of a spelling primer. (Four years later, in an effort to simply the teaching process, the missionaries would delete five consonants, leaving an alphabet of only five vowels and seven consonants.) Once spelling rules had been agreed upon, work began on the translation of the Bible, the different books being parceled out among the members of the company. It was not a work quickly done, even with reinforcements from later-arriving missionary companies: the New Testament was completed in 1832, the entire Bible in 1839.

All the while the work of preaching and teaching went forward. Despite Liholiho's initial hesitation, the Hawaiians warmed to this new breed of foreigners who behaved so differently from the other *haole* who had lived amongst them for a quarter century. Many of the alii, who over the years had become increasingly distraught over the effects of the foreign element on the kingdom, soon rallied to the missionary cause, and were the bulk of their early conversions; this was especially true of the women chiefs, in part because they could see that Christianity offered them an improved status in society. And for the alii in general Christianity became a rallying point for restoring a balance against the power of the king. Before its probationary year had expired the Pioneer Company had been granted permission to stay indefinitely, and the kingdom had requested that more companies be sent. In the ensuing quarter century the American Board of Commissioners for Foreign Missions would send eleven more companies to the islands. The impact these 150-odd men and women would have on Hawaii's future was prodigious: having arrived in a kingdom without a single school, within a decade the missionaries had established over a thousand throughout the islands, in the process bringing literacy to the majority of the Hawaiian people.

Apart from their work in conversion and its necessary counterpart, education, the missionaries had always intended to bring "Christian civilization" to the natives—indeed, they could hardly conceive of the first without the other. And from the missionaries' point of view, Hawaii was fertile ground much in need of cultivation and judicious weeding. The kapu system had been overthrown before their arrival, so at least they need not compete with an existing idolatrous religion; but infanticide, incest, polygamy, and extramarital sex were commonplace, as were drunkenness, gambling, "lewd dancing" (the hula), and public nudity. The missionaries fought them all, with varying degrees of success (and in the process introduced the forerunner of that delightful Hawaiian garment, the muumuu).

Not surprisingly, it was this moral campaign—increasingly reflected in the kingdom's laws, as the alii embraced Christian morality—that brought the missionaries into conflict with the whalers and the local traders and merchants who catered to them. It was the most basic of conflicts, between two opposing moral codes, made all the more acute, perhaps, by the missionaries' self-righteous manner. It fueled an antagonism between the two groups which would endure long into Hawaii's history.

Indeed, even in the modern era the missionaries are equated by some with colonizers, colonizers who moreover destroyed the Hawaiian culture. It is undoubtedly true that the missionaries' presence and morality had a profound impact on Hawaii, and that some aspects of the culture today regarded as positive (such as the hula) suffered along with others best forgotten. But the missionaries were a small contingent among a much larger foreign population, and few who have studied the record can doubt of their good intentions toward the islanders. Practically alone among those who came to the islands in that era they distinguished themselves in coming only for what they perceived to be the good of the Hawaiian people. It is well to remember that the missionaries acted in an era when "native ways" were more likely to be regarded as an affliction to be cured, rather than an identity to be preserved. As others have written before, if Hawaii's missionaries were colonizers, they were the most loving colonizers a society ever suffered.

And yet in one vital area the missionary effort would prove a failure. Crucial to the "Christian civilization" they envisioned was a dedication to hard work—"industry," as they called it—and the material rewards that industry would bring. But their successes in the spiritual and educational realms did not have their counterpart in the economic: indeed, by the mid-1830s it was clear that Hawaii was in an alarming long-term decline. Early visitors to the islands had commented on the bounty of the islands and the natives' capacity for hard work. But the missionaries were witnessing a very different Hawaii: idlers and drunkards in the towns, an alarming decrease in the native population, widespread hunger, and great expanses of fertile land left uncultivated. What had happened?

Several causes contributed: the inadvertent introduction of new epidemic diseases, the overthrow of the kapu system, the general breakdown of the authority of the alii, the abuses during the sandalwood era, and the example set by foreigners in the port towns. But many saw two factors as fundamental: the traditional, feudal property system under which all land was the property of the king and the alii, which contributed to the second—the Hawaiian preferred the simple pleasures of an easygoing existence with few possessions, to a life of struggle with more of them.

Whatever the causes, from the perspective of the mid-1830s, the future of the kingdom was a bleak one unless some unforeseen development intervened. What was the answer?

World Transformed:
from Kingdom
to King Sugar

Sugar.

Sugar cane was not new to Hawaii—the journals of Captain Cook's voyages had noted its cultivation in the islands; it had come with the ancient Hawaiians on their great voyages from the southern Pacific centuries before. But it had always been a minor crop, an occasional sweetener to a very limited diet. Since the turn of the century scattered attempts by Western immigrants to produce the crop commercially had met with failure. Then in 1835, the firm of Ladd & Company leased a large area at Koloa, Kauai, and established Hawaii's first successful sugar plantation (the plantation, under a different name and ownership, continues operating to this day).

Other plantations sprang up throughout the islands during the remainder of the decade (some 20 mills were reported to be in operation by 1838 alone, although this number soon fell as the efficiency of larger units became evident); the success of one venture encouraged another, and began to arouse a commercial spirit among chiefs and commoners alike. The former began planting their lands in cane for sale to the mills, while many commoners got their first taste of working for a money wage. The growth of sugar exports was equally impressive: from 8000 pounds in 1836, to 300,000 pounds ten years later. Acreage planted and exports alike would continue to grow slowly over the next fifteen years, when an event in far away America would bring about a spectacular increase in demand and production.

(Previous page): *A worker in the Oahu Sugar Company's Waipahu Factory holds a fresh batch of raw sugar.*
From halting beginnings in 1835, when the first successful sugar plantation was founded at Koloa, Kauai, the Hawaiian sugar industry grew throughout the 19th Century, receiving a huge boost when the American Civil War cut off Southern sugar. With miles of hand-dug ditches and tunnels (as the one shown *this page on Maui) the sugar men planted and irrigated cane on land previously thought unusable.*
With a native population in decline, the planters looked abroad for manpower, importing thousands of workers first from China, and later Japan (this page). *[Black and white photographs: Hawaii State Archives]*

But as sugar production expanded it became increasingly clear to the planters that they faced two serious problems which needed resolution. The islands were well-suited to the growing of cane, and with the construction of irrigation ditches and tunnels even the drier leeward slopes of the islands could be brought into production. But the planters did not own their land; they leased it from the king or the alii, who owned virtually all the land in the kingdom under the traditional landholding system—and no planter would be willing to sink large investments into rented land. The second problem was an inadequate labor supply: not only was the population of the islands insufficient and decreasing (the native population was in tragic decline: from an estimated 250,000 at the turn of the century, to approximately 100,000 in 1840); many of the native Hawaiians were unwilling to do the backbreaking work of the plantations.

To solve these problems the planters took the same approach that foreigners had taken since their earliest days in the kingdom: they began pressing for fundamental change. In fact, to a large extent the story of 19th Century Hawaii, particularly from 1840 on, is just that: the relentless demands of a growing foreign population for changes in the system to suit their needs. Often as not the result, if not the intention, was to the disadvantage of the native population.

In this instance the pressure from the sugar industry helped produce two far-reaching developments. The labor problem was solved by

turning to the large-scale importation of contract labor: in 1852 some 300 Chinese workers arrived. Over the next quarter century thousands more followed, until, fearful of being overrun by Chinese immigrants, the planters turned to other nationalities: Portuguese, German, Puerto Rican, Japanese, and, later, Filipinos.

With respect to the land issue, the planters merely added their voice to what had become, over an extended time, a widespread demand for a reform of the land system. The result became known as the Great Mahele ("division").

As we have seen, from ancient times all the land of Hawaii was the property of the kings, who distributed it in fief among the alii; they in turn parceled out the use of small farm plots to the commoners. As foreigners settled in growing numbers in the islands this traditional system was the source of ever-increasing conflict, since they were accustomed to the right of outright ownership of land. The missionaries, too, came to feel that the commoners would never develop the virtues of industry and responsibility without individual ownership of their kuleanas. And lastly the alii would stand to benefit by a determination of their absolute right to property, as opposed to holding land at the pleasure of the king.

In 1848 the king and government responded to these pressures by enacting a division of the land of the kingdom. The process was a lengthy and fairly complex one, but the end result can be summarized fairly succinctly: from the division the king personally retained as "Crown Lands" about 1,000,000 acres; the alii, about 1,500,000 acres; the government, about 1,500,000 acres; and the commoners, about 30,000 acres. (The result was not quite as lopsided as it appears, since the kuleanas granted to the commoners was nearly always valuable farm land, while a large portion of the other grants consisted of mountainous or lava wasteland without agricultural value.) In 1850 this revolution in the land tenure system was completed—much to the satisfaction of the planters— by granting aliens the right to buy land. (Despite the good intentions, the Great Mahele would eventually come to be seen as a disaster for the Hawaiian people.

Sugar brought a new wealth to
Hawaii: in 1879 King Kalakaua
began construction of a magnificent
new palace, the Iolani (opposite); but
sugar also helped create a powerful
pro-American white community
increasingly at odds with the
monarchy. In 1893 they deposed
Queen Liliuokalani (this page) and
petitioned the United States for
annexation. Rebuffed by the
Cleveland Administration in
Washington, they established the
Republic of Hawaii. [Liliuokalani
photograph: Bishop Museum]

Pearl Harbor's potential as a naval base had attracted the attention of the United States since the 1840s, when a young naval officer named Charles Wilkes led an expedition to reconnoiter the Pacific. For the remainder of the century the United States periodically debated the strategic value of the islands. When the Spanish-American War erupted in 1898, America decided annexation of Hawaii was a good idea after all.

Those who condemned the traditional land system saw only its faults; but it provided a stable foundation for those who had always worked the land and knew no other way of life. Once the commoner had outright ownership of his land he was also free to sell it, and many did, for quick money or to pay debts, and thus lost the underpinnings of their security.)

With land and labor problems resolved, the sugar industry could go forward; and just in time, for with the start of the California Gold Rush in 1848, and the American Civil War in 1860, demand for Hawaii's sugar boomed, with exports increasing more than ten-fold between 1860 and 1866. (Coincidentally, the naval depredations of the Civil War—and the discovery of oil in Pennsylvania in 1859—was killing off the whaling industry.) Ten years later a treaty with the United States for duty-free entry of Hawaiian sugar would see another explosion in production and exports. By this point virtually every suitable acre of the islands was planted to cane; sugar's transformation of the Hawaiian landscape was complete.

Since the sugar industry was virtually the creature of the islands' foreigners, as the industry had grown, so did their economic power; not surprisingly, this power was increasingly felt in the political sphere as well.

Indeed, one could well argue that Hawaii's history since the day Captain Cook sailed over the horizon had been a continuing reaction and adjustment to foreign influence. For an entity so small, so fragile, perhaps it could hardly have been otherwise, given the power of the outside world. The rise of King Kamehameha I, and his unification of the kingdom, owed much to Western technology; but in general Kamehameha was master of, rather than mastered by, the white man. His successors were not so fortunate.

For as is often the case with those who follow a great leader, the kings who followed Kamehameha I paled in comparison. His son, Liholiho (Kamehameha II), who had developed a strong attachment for the English and their King George IV, sailed for London on a state visit in 1823, only four years into his reign, and only to die there of measles the following year. When news of Liholiho's death reached Honolulu some months later, his ten-year-old brother, Kauikeaouli (Kamehameha III), ascended the throne, initially under the regency of Kaahumanu. His reign would stretch over 30 years—the longest in Hawaiian history—ending with his death in 1854. But it sometimes seemed that both kings were more interested in the trappings of monarchy than in the discipline, hard work, and hard decisions of governing a kingdom.

Thus a number of circumstances combined after 1819 to diminish the stature and power of the monarchy which Kamehameha I had established. The overthrow of the kapu system immediately following his death was obviously the first momentous consequence—and a harbinger of the influence that Western man and his ideas would have on the kingdom throughout the remainder of the 19th Century. For the monarchs who followed Kamehameha the Great, life must often have seemed an endless struggle with the *haole*, the white men, who behaved as though it was they, rather than the Hawaiians, who best knew how to rule the islands.

Nonetheless, in the earliest struggles over the monarchical power following Kamehameha's death, the foreign community was only indirectly involved; instead, it was the chiefs, whose power had been greatly diminished under Kamehameha, who moved to re-establish their traditional position. Whether from principle or expedience, the chiefs rallied around the standard of the Christian morality preached by the missionaries, in opposition to the tendencies of Liholiho and Kauikeaouli, both of whom showed a preference for the "good life" as lived by the traders and whalemen. The result, during the 1820s and 30s, was the evolution of a council of chiefs which effectively limited the king's power, and which planted the seed of representative government. That seed was nurtured with the constitution of 1840, which created a legislative body whose lower house was to consist of popular representatives. Needless to say, what underlay much of this evolution—what were, in fact, indispensable to it—were the philosophical concepts the missionaries and other foreigners brought to the kingdom: the individual dignity and equality of man, the rule of law, and democracy.

As the century wore on, more and more foreigners were drawn to the kingdom, and as their numbers increased and the economy developed, pressures for representative, progressive government grew apace: in 1852 a new constitution was promulgated, creating a lower house elected by direct vote of all male citizens.

What also evolved was a divide between the the the white, foreign-born community and the native Hawaiians. The interests of the former lay with development of sugar and trade, the free importation of contract labor, and the minimum of cost and interference from government. Meanwhile the Hawaiians saw their land, their islands, being slowly taken over by people who in some cases had arrived only a few years before. Further, their own population was steadily diminishing; not surprisingly, they increasingly began to see their salvation in a strong monarchy House of Nobles appointed by the king.

When Lot (Kamehameha V), the last of the Kamehamehas (Kamehameha IV had succeeded Kamehameha III in 1854) ascended to the throne in 1863, he brought this conflict into the open by abrogating the constitution of 1852 and promulgating the constitution of 1864, in which the powers of the monarchy and the House of Nobles were greatly enhanced. Lot meant to restore the power of the Hawaiian monarchy, and in so doing, restore the Hawaiian people to their rightful place in the kingdom.

For nearly 25 years, and two more kings (Lunalilo, the first of Hawaii's kings to be elected by the legislature, reigned only briefly, having died in 1874, a year after ascending the throne; and David Kalakaua, king during 1874-91), the situation festered. But the forces of demographics and economics were working against the Hawaiians: as their own population grew smaller and poorer, the whites grew more numerous and richer. From the 1860s on the sugar planters were virtually the entire economy—and thus the tax base—of the islands. Adding fuel to the fire were King Kalakaua's interests and spending habits: bent on enhancing the glory of the monarchy and restoring the traditional Hawaiian culture (his love of the hula and celebrations earned him the nickname "Merrie Monarch"), he spent lavishly on entertainments and a palace fit for a king, the Iolani.

Finally the planters and their allies had had enough:

in the bloodless "Revolution of 1887" Kalakaua was forced to accept a new constitution which reduced him to the status of ceremonial monarch. But this was not all: through income and property qualifications for voting, the new constitution effectively disenfranchised the majority of the Hawaiian people, while ensuring votes to people of means. Most people of means, as it turned out, were white foreigners.

But gaining effective control of the government solved only one of the planters' problems, and not the most important one at that: despite a Reciprocity Treaty signed in 1876 providing for duty-free entry of Hawaiian sugar into the United States, each swing of mood over sugar policy in the American congress gave the planters the jitters. What Hawaii really needed, the planters knew, was a guarantee of access to the American market; what was really needed, the planters were beginning to think, was annexation to the United States.

It was by no means the first time the idea had arisen; as early as mid-century, and again in 1873, the idea of leasing or selling Pearl Harbor to the United States for a naval base had been suggested. (In 1887 the idea was put into effect, when the United States was granted exclusive rights to the use of Pearl Harbor as part of the "package" renewing the Reciprocity Treaty.) And as both contacts with America and the number of resident Americans had increased throughout the 19th Century, the discussion of some sort of eventual union was a natural consequence. But now such discussion had a more serious tone: big money, and the kingdom's very prosperity, were at stake.

But it was not a discussion in which the Hawaiians, and especially the Hawaiian royalty, had much in common with the Americans. For them such a move would be the ultimate capitulation: they had lost their land, they had lost most of their people—now they were being asked to surrender the last symbol of their identity, their kingdom.

In 1891, with the death of Kalakaua, his sister, Liliuokalani, the first ruling queen in Hawaiian history, came to the throne. She would also be Hawaii's last monarch. For like Kalakaua, Liliuokalani wanted to rule, rather than merely reign over, Hawaii. In early 1893 she adjourned the legislature and proposed a new constitution which restored the monarchy's independent powers and under which only "true Hawaiians" could vote. For the annexationists, who had formed themselves into an armed Committee of Safety, this was the last straw: calling upon the aid of troops aboard an American warship in port, they occupied downtown Honolulu, where they read a proclamation announcing the end of the monarchy and the birth of a provisional government. Liliuokalani's troops, apparently seeing the futility of resistance, quickly lay down their arms. It was the death knell of the Hawaiian monarchy.

The new government immediately proposed union with the United States, only to be rejected by the newly elected Cleveland administration; undaunted, the revolutionaries promulgated the Republic of Hawaii in 1894, and waited for a change of heart in Washington. A year later the royalists attempted a counterrevolution which was quickly suppressed; Liliuokalani was placed under house arrest in Iolani Palace and forced to sign a formal abdication renouncing all claims to the monarchy. (She was released later that year and restored to full citizenship in November of 1896.)

In the end it was the outbreak in 1898 of the Spanish-American War—itself a by-product of "manifest destiny"—which convinced the U.S. Congress of the advantages of having Hawaii and Pearl Harbor under the American flag. On August 12 of that year Hawaii formally became part of U.S. territory, and with the formation of a territorial government in 1900, control by the white community was all but complete, since it was their voices which were best heard in Washington, in the (Washington-appointed) governor's office, and, to a lesser extent, in the territorial legislature.

With worries about an assured market laid to rest, the sugar planters could pull out all the stops on investment. Sugar acreage, production, and exports began an inexorable climb. One thing that did not increase was the number of firms in the industry, for economy of scale continued to assert itself, resulting in a steady concentration of the industry into a handful of firms which came to be called the "Big Five": Alexander & Baldwin, American Factors, Castle & Cooke, C. Brewer & Co., and Theo. Davies & Co. For the most part originating as financing and marketing companies in the latter half of the 19th Century, by 1910 these firms controlled three quarters of the sugar crop; 20 years later, virtually the entirety. As the century wore on the Big Five would branch out from their sugar bases, eventually dominating all aspects of the Hawaiian economy.

With increased sugar production came too the continued need for a steady supply of labor, and since

Pilot Bob Stuhr takes a self-portrait as his crop-duster rises from a pass over a cane field on the McBryde plantation at Koloa, Kauai, the oldest in Hawaii. By continually applying new technology and modernizing aging factories (this page), Hawaii's sugar industry has been able to maintain production at high levels despite shrinking acreage. But the era when "King Sugar" ruled Hawaii did not long survive in the post-war period, as labor unions for the first time organized effectively and the economy diversified into other areas.

The decline in sugar acreage and employment since World War II has been accompanied by the growth in tourism, and in some cases the relics of the sugar era have been converted into tourist attractions. At Koloa, the birthplace of the industry, the plantation town has been rescued from slow deterioration by converting it into a tourist-oriented shopping center (opposite). On Maui's Kaanapali Coast the steam rail line once used to haul cane to the Pioneer Mill now offers Lahaina visitors a nostalgic ride (this page).

Some aspects of the sugar industry seem virtually unchanged from decades past. Although most field operations, including harvesting, are heavily mechanized, for some tasks a man and machete are unmatched—so on the McBryde plantation on Kauai, Wilson Campos still hand-cuts "seed" cane, from which the new crop is grown (this page). Despite continuous modernization, Hawaii's sugar industry—with the highest agricultural labor wages in the world—operates at a severe disadvantage to foreign producers; for workers like Wilson and Arcadio Cadiz (opposite), a mechanic at Hawaiian Commercial & Sugar Company's Puunene factory on Maui, the future is cloudy indeed.

immigrant workers routinely left the plantations for other work when their contracts were up, this meant the need for a continued immigrant flow. Japan had replaced China as the primary labor source in the 1880s, and by 1907, when the flow of contract laborers from Japan was cut off (picture brides were still permitted entry until 1924, when all Oriental immigration into the United States was halted by legislation), there were some 100,000 Japanese in the islands. When the Japanese supply was cut off, the planters turned to the Philippines, which, thanks to the Spanish-American War, was also under the U.S. flag, and by the 1930s well over half the work force of the plantations was Filipino.

At the opening of the century, then, Hawaii's planters enjoyed near-perfect conditions for sugar production and marketing: the day of "King Sugar" had arrived. (And, with James D. Dole's successful introduction of pineapple cultivation in 1901, the islands found an ideal complement to sugar cultivation for areas too dry or too far from an adequate water source to grow sugar cane.) And for the first three decades of the century it appeared that this near-perfect plantation economy might endure indefinitely. Then in 1934 the Jones-Costigan Act, passed by Congress for the benefit of mainland sugar producers, categorized Hawaiian sugar with foreign producers, and reduced Hawaii's import quota. Passage of the law made the planters newly aware of the fragility of a territory's politico-economic situation; henceforward many joined their voices to those who had long advocated statehood for Hawaii.

But another factor was also at work, in less dramatic fashion, which meant that the days of domination by the white plantocracy were numbered: while the immigrant contract labor force had long been virtually without political power due to their alien status and lack of education, under American law their Hawaii-born children were automatically citizens, and went to school, in English. As they came of age, their voices—and votes—would increasingly be heard. To hurry the process along, in the late 1930s union officials from the mainland began organizing in the islands, beginning with the longshoremen and shipping companies. Their early efforts produced some violent clashes with employers bent on keeping out "outside agitators," but as 1941 was drawing to a close, they had nearly completed organizing the islands' ports. The plantation workers could not be far behind.

Today's World: Sun, Sand and Statehood

Japan's attack on Pearl Harbor the morning of December 7, 1941 (opposite), plunged America into World War II and Hawaii into martial law. For Hawaii's large Japanese-American population the battlefield exploits of the famed "442nd"—a highly-decorated regiment of Japanese-American soldiers—helped establish their "credentials" as equal citizens. (Veterans of the 442nd pose, this page, top in the Punchbowl—the National Memorial Cemetery of the Pacific—where a monument this page, bottom overlooks the final resting place of many of World War II's fallen.) [Pearl Harbor photograph: U.S. Army]

It goes without saying that the war that came to America on the Sunday morning of December 7, 1941 deeply affected the entire country; but nowhere did World War II have a deeper impact than in Hawaii. First there was the fact of the Pearl Harbor attack itself, in which nearly 2400 people—including more than 50 civilians—were killed. Isolated in mid-Pacific, people in Hawaii doubtless had greater reason to fear further attacks than those on the mainland. And Hawaii, unlike the mainland, was subjected to martial law, which was not lifted until the war was almost over.

What made Hawaii special in the eyes of military authorities, apart from its geographical vulnerability and the fact of the attack, was its large population of Japanese, both resident alien and citizen. (On the eve of the war Hawaii's Japanese numbered more than 150,000—over one third of the population. Questions about their true loyalties had been raised, especially on the mainland, for a decade before the outbreak of the war.) In the climate of the moment and the times martial law was considered the minimum step essential to Hawaii's security; on the Pacific coast of the mainland, citizens and aliens of Japanese ancestry were interned or forced to relocate to the interior of the country. But the sheer numbers of Japanese in Hawaii made such a step impractical. (Thousands were interrogated by loyalty boards, and in the end nearly 1500 people, most of them Japanese,

Dating from 1927, the Royal Hawaiian Hotel remains Waikiki's most famous man-made landmark (this page). Built by the Matson Navigation Company to accommodate the passengers on its legendary liners, the "Pink Palace" still evokes the glory days of Hawaii's tourism. Early dawn light silhouettes an even more famous landmark, the profile of Diamond Head (opposite). To the Hawaiians the extinct crater was Lae 'ahi ("brow of the 'ahi fish"); early 19th-Century British sailors coined the name when they dis-covered rocks with diamond-like crystals on its slopes.

Completed in 1969, ten years after Hawaii became the 50th State in the Union, the Capitol (opposite) houses both the legislative and executive branches in a building suggesting volcanoes rising out of the sea. With the 1986 inauguration of John Waihee (shown, this page, on the grounds of Washington Place, the official residence, with his wife Lynne), Hawaii for the first time had an elected Governor of Hawaiian ancestry.

The development of large long-distance passenger aircraft in the 50s and 60s put Hawaii within geographical and financial reach of mass tourism; the subsequent explosion of visitor arrivals (from 320,000 in 1961 to nearly 2 million ten years later) transformed Waikiki's 600-odd acres into a forest of high-rise hotels and condominiums (opposite).

were interned at island or mainland camps. In the end, only one person—a German—was convicted of espionage in Hawaii during the war.)

Martial law weighed heavily on the islands, not only for the inconvenience and inequities it caused generally (most Hawaiian residents were required to remain at their pre-attack jobs, while thousands of mainlanders came in and took high-paying defense work), but for the aspersion it cast on the Japanese population. Surveillance was widespread, beaches were closed, a dusk-to-dawn curfew was imposed, towns and countryside went dark under a blackout order.

Initially the wartime authorities were unsure of what to do with Hawaii's Japanese of military age, but as the war developed it became obvious that every man available would be needed for the fighting. Eventually the Army issued a call for an all-Japanese fighting unit, to be denominated the 442nd Infantry Regiment: within weeks the unit had over 9000 volunteers. After training, the unit was sent to the European theatre, where other all-Japanese units, including the 100th Battalion (formed earlier from the Hawaiian National Guard) and mainland volunteers, were absorbed into the 442nd. Fighting in France and Italy, the 442nd quickly became one of the most famous units in the U.S. forces, taking one of the highest casualty rates in the Army. When the war came to a close in the summer of 1945 the 442nd had become one of the most highly decorated units in American history.

For the young Japanese and thousands of other islanders who served, the war was a great eye-opener: many had never before visited the mainland, much less any other part of the world. When they came back to Hawaii at war's end they returned with a new sense of their American-ness. They would soon add their weight to the political scene and the drive for statehood.

For Hawaii's Japanese the war had added to the psychological burden which years of questions about divided loyalties had imposed. Now the wartime exploits of their sons had done much to lift that burden, erasing for all time any doubts about their "full citizenship" as Americans. And the war did something else as well: it provided the rallying point for political organization. One could well argue that, even without the war's intervention, the Japanese were ripe for moving into political power: by the 1940s they constituted over a third of the population, although their percentage of voters was less. But the war obviously provided opportunities for leaders to distinguish themselves, and it gave them a chance to prove, even to themselves, that they were as good as anybody. In the post-war years Japanese veterans moved into positions of leadership in a Democratic Party which had come to see that its chance to unseat the Republican Party—long the bastion of the Big Five and their allies—lay in assembling a coalition of the territory's minorities. With each post-war election, Japanese representation in the territorial legislature increased; with the 1954 election, over half the members of both houses were AJAs—Americans of Japanese Ancestry. (The same year would see the Democratic Party oust the Republicans from control of the legislature—a domination which has continued to the present day.)

The war would prove a big boost for the cause of statehood as well. For one thing, the people of Hawaii came through the war with a new sense of belonging to the American nation (although, when it came to that, there seemed little need of convincing:

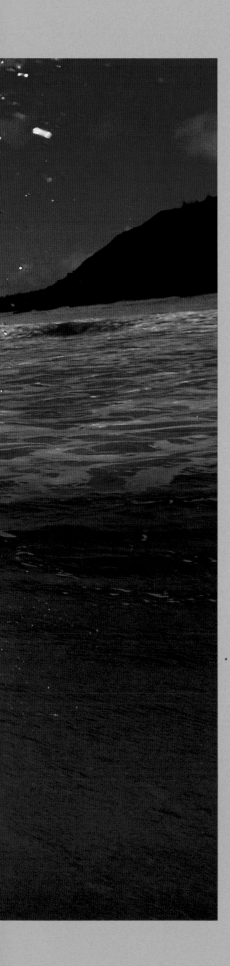

An invention of the ancient Hawaiians, who called it he'e nalu ("wave sliding"), Hawaiian surfing gained international fame during the 30s and 40s when Hawaii's legendary swimmer, Olympic gold medalist Duke Kahanamoku, championed the sport. The huge winter waves which frequently pound Oahu's North Shore have made it one of the world's great surfing meccas.

Hawaii's constant summer-like climate, coupled with Maui's famed "breezes" draw the world's premier windsurfers to that island year-round.

as far back as 1940 Hawaiians had voted overwhelmingly in favor of statehood). The real issue was mainland attitudes—and here, too, the attack on Pearl Harbor and Hawaii's role in the war helped convince Americans that Hawaii and its people were a part of the nation, even if separated from the mainland. Then too, in the half-century to the 1950s Hawaii had become a very different place: at annexation over half the population had been aliens; now aliens counted for less than ten percent of the total. Other factors were operating in favor of statehood as well: thousands of mainlanders had spent a part of the war in Hawaii, thus seeing for themselves that the islands, however far away, were thoroughly Americanized; the same went for tourists both before and after the war; America was becoming more aware of its own racial and ethnic diversity; and technology, in the form of the airplane and telecommunications, were bringing the islands nearer. With the admission of Alaska as the 49th State of the Union in 1958, the issue of lack of contiguity to the mainland, perhaps the biggest obstacle of all, was dealt a heavy blow. The following year the U.S. House and Senate acted, and on August 21, 1959, Hawaii officially entered the Union as its 50th State.

As Hawaii was entering the age of statehood, the world was entering a new age as well: the jet age. And with the arrival of long-distance air travel (actually ushered in a few years before with propeller-driven long-distance passenger aircraft), Hawaii was about to enter its era as a destination of mass tourism.

Tourism was not new to Hawaii; since the turn of the century and even before, the islands had been visited by vacationers—among them famous writers such as Mark Twain, Robert Louis Stevenson, and Jack London, each of whom had recorded his thoughts about Hawaii's exotic splendors. Matson steamers such as the *Lurline, Mariposa, and Malolo* became famous in the early decades of this century plying their run between Honolulu and San Francisco. A few hotels, the most famous of which were Waikiki's

Every other summer Honolulu is host to yachts completing the California-to-Hawaii Transpacific Yacht Race, first held in 1906 (in the photograph opposite *finishers from the 1986 "Trans-Pac" warm up for a follow-on around-Oahu race); polo, here being played at the Mokuleia field on Oahu's North Shore, has been a part of Hawaii's sporting scene since before the turn of the century (this page).*

Home port to ships of the U.S. Pacific Fleet, Pearl Harbor (opposite) is just part of a massive American military presence in the islands, most of it concentrated on Oahu. (A quarter of Oahu's land area is under military ownership or control.) The Army, Air Force, and Marine Corps also maintain sizable bases, and the total of military personnel and dependents constitutes more than ten percent of the State's population.

Ironically, "Pearl Harbor Day" ensured that the base would become a major tourist attraction as well. Since its dedication in 1962, the Arizona Memorial has become, after the Punchbowl's memorial cemetery, Hawaii's most-visited tourist destination. Every year well over a million visitors pilgrimage to the monument commemorating the eleven hundred officers and men lost in the sinking of the battleship (this page).

With the filling up of Waikiki and the increasing number of repeat visitors to the State, the neighbor islands have received a growing share of tourist arrivals. The latest trend has been to immense, self-contained vacation complexes, such as the spectacular one overlooking Kauai's Nawiliwili Bay (following pages).

Moana (opened in 1901), Halekulani (1917), and the Royal Hawaiian (1927), were available to accommodate these visitors. But such travel was a luxury, available only to the wealthy or the professional traveler; few but they could afford the cost and time involved for a sojourn whose sea portion alone would consume five days each way.

After the war, the airplane and a period of unparalleled U.S. prosperity combined to transform Hawaii from a distant sleepy outpost known mainly for its sugar and pineapples, into America's most famous vacation State. Perhaps vacation "spot" would be more apt, for in the early years "Hawaii" to the tourist meant "Waikiki," and hotel after hotel rose on its 600-odd acres, to house the growing influx of visitors (some 300,000 in 1961, nearly two million in 1971, and just under four million ten years later). All those bodies browning in the sun meant big money, and in the early 1980s tourism became the largest contributor to the State's economy. It was not, however, agriculture which tourism surpassed to gain the number one spot. In the early 1950s federal government outlays (defense and civilian combined) had already surpassed agriculture in importance to the economy, and the persistence of the Cold War into the modern era ensured a continuous large military presence at Pearl Harbor and other bases in the islands. (Military spending during World War II had, of course, temporarily mushroomed out of all proportion to other sectors.)

Although agricultural production remained at high levels in the postwar period, with cane production exceeding ten million tons throughout the 60s, it was obvious that the heyday of sugar and pineapple were numbered. The same forces that had brought Hawaii into the modern age had changed the conditions under which the plantations had flourished: unionization and the cut-off of contract labor immigration made wages and working conditions the envy of the world, but steadily reduced the price-competitiveness of Hawaii's sugar and pineapple, despite a fierce pace of mechanization. From the 60s onward both sugar and pineapple land were being taken out of production, and the number of mills operating, and workers employed, shrank repeatedly. To some extent the decline in agriculture has been moderated by turning to crop diversification, such as macadamia nuts, papaya, and flower growing. But the most significant "crop diversification" of all for the Big Five and other large landowners has been the development of their land into extensive tourist resorts, such as the Kaanapali and Wailea areas on Maui, and the Kona coast of Hawaii.

The post-war era also saw a rapid growth in population and urbanization, resulting in part from the steady flow of workers off the plantations and a large in-migration of mainlanders, especially from the 1960s onward. (So large in fact, that by 1980 the white population had surpassed the Japanese as the largest ethnic group in the islands; in the same year the overall population of the islands was just under one million, having nearly doubled since 1950.) These factors accelerated the steady integration of the islands into the American "mainstream," a process which eventually brought the realization that the islands were in danger of losing those elements of Hawaiian culture which had always made the islands a special place.

One result was a reawakening of interest in many aspects of Hawaiian culture, a movement which came to be known as the "Hawaiian Renaissance." All manner of Hawaiians, from every ethnic group, took up the study of the Hawaiian language, history, or a traditional skill such as hula, lei making, quilting, or canoe building. As a part-Hawaiian I came to know on the island of Hawaii told me, the Hawaiian Renaissance was in essence a form of aloha. "I don't mean just a word the tourist promoters latched onto, but the real aloha. One of the meanings of 'aloha' is love," she remarked. "To me, those who have taken the Hawaiian Renaissance into their hearts are expressing a love for the Hawaiian culture, and through the culture, for the Hawaiian people and these islands. Hawaii has seen a lot of change over the last two hundred years, not all of it for the good, and certainly not all of it for the good of my people. Despite what the guide books say, it is not always an interracial paradise—but, for all and all, I think there has always been a good measure of true aloha, of regard for one another, a willingness to overlook faults and go on. Hawaii for a time was maybe forgetting that aloha; the Hawaiian Renaissance, as they call it, helped remind all us that it is aloha that makes Hawaii such a special place. I can't imagine Hawaii without it, and it's because of aloha—the aloha spirit, if you want to call it that—that I wouldn't live anywhere else."

Hawaiian Heart

At the forefront of efforts to conserve and explain Hawaii's past, as well as to promote its traditional, living culture, are a handful of museums throughout the islands. The largest and most famous of these is Honolulu's Bernice Pauahi Bishop Museum (opposite), founded in 1889 by Charles Reed Bishop as a memorial to his wife, the last surviving direct descendant of King Kamehameha I. The museum houses the world's premier collections of Hawaiian and Pacific artifacts, as well as offering ongoing classes in a number of Hawaiian crafts.

The collection of a neighbor island museum includes a superb anthropomorphic stone carving (this page) dug up in a cane field in 1930. Very likely a "house god" belonging to a person of rank, the detailed working of the stone suggests a "post-contact" origin, since metal was unknown to the islands prior to the European discovery. Although religious idols were ordered destroyed after the overthrow of the kapu system in 1819, it is known that many Hawaiians retained a strong belief in the traditional religious system, and secreted away the icons of their faith. [Icon height 10 inches: museum collection (Hawaiian Islands), anonymous by request]

The cotton plant was unknown to the ancient Hawaiians, and prior to Western contact the only cloth utilized was kapa, pounded from the bark of the paper mulberry (wauke). With the arrival of the Protestant missionaries in the 1820s came the first permanent resident Western women, and with them the art of quilting. Both cotton cloth and quilting caught on quickly with the Hawaiians, and the latter soon established itself as a favorite handicraft, as kapa died out (kapa-making is today virtually unknown in Hawaii; modern examples are almost invariably imports from Polynesia of the southern Pacific). "Auntie" Debbie Kakalia

(pictured above) is recognized as one of a handful of Hawaii's master quilters, and teaches her craft both privately and at the Bishop Museum. Each quilt requires scores of hours of work, and would sell for several hundred dollars each, but Auntie Debbie almost never produces a quilt for sale, preferring to present them as special gifts to people whom she admires. Pictured (opposite, top row and bottom left) are three of her designs, together with an historic "Flag Quilt," by an unknown quilter, from a neighbor island museum collection (museum anonymous by request).

No visitor to Hawaii spends long in the islands before noticing outrigger canoes (opposite), and no Hawaiian tradition has longer roots than what is today both a craft and sport. The canoes usually seen today are those for competition or practice, forty feet long, constructed of Fibreglas, and carrying six paddlers. Some 45 canoe clubs throughout the islands bring together men, women, and youngsters with an interest in both sport and preserving an ancient Hawaiian heritage. The racing season begins in the spring, and includes some annual classics, the most renowned of which is the grueling Molokai-to-Oahu race held in October.

It was of course in canoes that the first Polynesians reached Hawaii, giant twin-hulled canoes fashioned of hollowed-out tree trunks, joined by a central platform, and powered by both paddlers and sails of bark cloth.

Although such canoes have not been built since the early 1800s, the tradition of wooden canoes is kept alive by dedicated craftsmen such as Wright Bowman and his assistants, shown working (this page) on a canoe of native koa in the canoe shed of the Kamehameha Schools. (In 1985 the Hokule'a, a sixty-foot recreation of an historic voyaging canoe, set out from Hawaii on a "Voyage of Rediscovery" to the south Pacific, with the intent of demonstrating the ability of such craft and crew to traverse long ocean stretches against prevailing winds, using only the navigational techniques known to the ancient Polynesians—stars, wave patterns, and bird paths. Three years later, after visiting much of Polynesia, the craft and international crew made a triumphant return to Hawaii.)

Today the most famous of Hawaii's musical instruments, the ukulele (oo-koo-LAY-lay) has a relatively short Hawaiian history, having been introduced to the islands by Portuguese immigrants from Madeira (and derived from their braguinha) in 1879. James Haluapo (opposite) sands an instrument in the only surviving ukulele factory in the islands, owned and managed by brothers Sam and Fred Kamaka. "There were still four companies until sometime after the Second World War," Sam Kamaka told me on a visit to the Honolulu factory. "But like a lot of other things, there has been a consolidation over the years. Except for a few artisans who hand-craft a few 'ukes,' we're the only ones left. 'Course, there's some mainland and foreign competition, especially at the low end of the market. We make around 5000 ukuleles a year, give or take. We used to make more—altogether, maybe half a million since my father started this business back in 1916." The factory makes four different sizes of the four-stringed instrument, up to the "baritone" model; a fully hand-made custom ukulele will have over 80 man-hours of labor, and may retail for over five hundred dollars. We were interrupted as a visiting group of fifth-graders trooped through on a field trip, escorted by Fred Kamaka. "We're happy to have them," Sam commented. "In part, we feel a sense of responsibility, to pass on knowledge of the 'uke. We don't want these kids growing up knowing only electric guitars and rock music. And it's not bad for business, either."

At a music school in nearby Aiea, four-year-old Bret Gamiao (this page) bends to the task of making his fingers into "jumping fleas"—which, when translated into Hawaiian, becomes, just as the instrument became, "ukulele."

"Leis are the fullest expression of 'aloha,' because they are for giving to one another. I think that's why the lei has survived as the most popular and best known of the traditional Hawaiian crafts." The speaker was Marie McDonald (pictured this page), in her workshop at Waimea on the Big Island, a part-Hawaiian who, with her husband, operates a nursery just outside the town. "The lei I'm doing now you'd never see in a lei shop—you would only get one on special order—they're simply too expensive for the usual retail market. They might take over an hour to create, and that's not counting the time spent gathering the flowers." Her lei pictured (this page, below) is a haku lei, created of roses, amaranth, Australian tea, veronica, liko lehua, statice, and leather fern.

Two hours away down the Kona coast, painter Herb Kawainui Kane (opposite) lives and works in the coffee country overlooking Kealakekua Bay, where two centuries ago Hawaii's Western discoverer, Captain Cook, died in the clash of cultures which was to dominate Hawaii's history for the next two centuries. As a part-Hawaiian who has lived a good part of his life outside Hawaii, it is thus perhaps no mere coincidence that Herb Kane has become the outstanding chronicler of Hawaiian history and culture, and especially of that crucial period just prior to and after Western contact. "I suppose living and working in a number of different places throughout my life has brought me face-to-face with the experience of adapting to different cultures. Of course, it's been nothing like the culture shock the Hawaiians lived through, but undoubtedly it made me more attuned to the ramifications both for the individual and society. Certainly my paintings try to capture the combination of bewilderment and wonder that must have filled that era, and the struggle for Hawaiians to hold on to their culture."

Although Hawaii's monarchy ceased to reign with the overthrow of Queen Liliuokalani in 1893, it is still remembered and honored with great fondness in the islands. Some of the most dramatic reminders of the royal era are the appearances of the various Hawaiian societies at Kawaiahao Church (shown opposite *are members of the Kaahumanu Society*). In their striking costume, accented by a unique, identifying lei or cape, the organizations gather for special Sunday services honoring noteworthy figures members of royalty or the alii class.

Had Hawaii's monarchy endured, the man who would very likely reign over the islands today is *Prince Edward Keliiahonui Kawananakoa* (this page), *the direct descendant of King Kalakaua's heir-designate. Prince Kawananakoa is posed in the Queen Emma Summer Palace before a portrait of Queen Emma's mother, Fanny Young Naea.*

Hawaii's biggest annual celebration of its heritage is Aloha Week, usually held in late September, and featuring a "Royal Court" and various cultural festivities on each island. The biggest of these events is Honolulu's Aloha Week parade through Waikiki (pictured in an overview of Kalakaua Avenue, opposite). A well-muscled royal standard-bearer jokes with his comrades (this page) as they wait for the parade to get under way.

Although the loss of and the continuing threat to Hawaii's heritage is justifiably a matter of concern, it is also undeniably true that Hawaii has managed to preserve its traditional, pre-European culture to a degree unapproached in any other part of America.

One of the spectacular features of Honolulu's Aloha Week parade are the pa'u (literally, 'skirt') riders: equestriennes in elaborate leis on equally-festooned mounts. Each of the eight large Hawaiian islands is represented by a troupe of riders wearing the lei and color of that island: Kauai—Mokihana/purple; Niihau—Pupu/white; Oahu—Ilima/ orange-yellow; Molokai—kukui/ silver-green; Lanai—Kaunaoa/orange; Maui—lokelani/pink; and Hawaii— lei lehua/red.

Although the horse was unknown to pre-contact Hawaii, after its introduction by Westerners in 1803 it quickly became a part of Hawaiian life, especially in managing wild range cattle. (Cattle had been introduced in the 1790s, and quickly multiplied under the protection of a royal kapu.) Hawaii retains a strong "horse culture," and weekend calf-roping contests and rodeos among amateur and professional paniolos (like the Kona Stampede opposite) are a common feature on all the islands.

Octogenarian Elizabeth Nalani Ellis (opposite) has been a member of the Kaahumanu Society for over thirty years, while five-year-old Marithel Battad (this page) is a brand-new member of a hula troupe performing for visitors to Honolulu's Ala Moana shopping center.

The profusion of tropical flowers is of course one of Hawaii's wonders. Among the most common, yet most beautiful, are the plumeria (this page), a favorite of lei makers; and the hibiscus, which hold their bloom for a single day and then wilt. On the opposite page are just four among hundreds of species (one of which, the red kokio 'ula, is the official flower of Hawaii).

Kauaʻi: a Lush Garden Wilderness

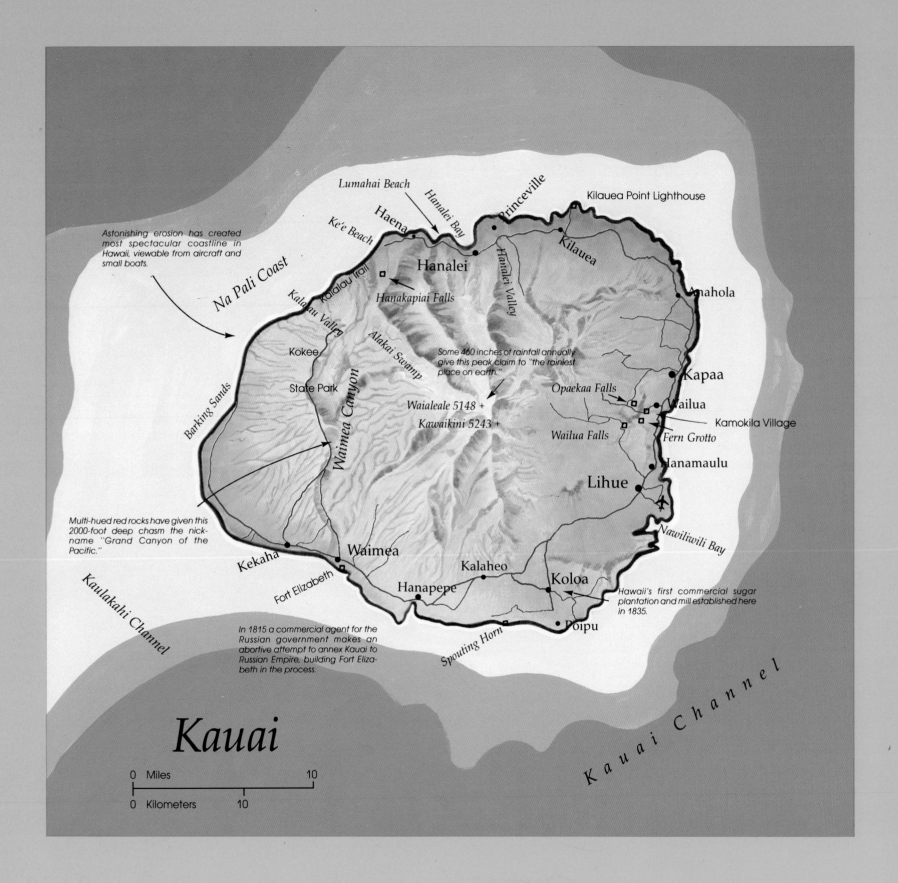

Lumahai Beach

Hanalei Bay

Princeville

Kilauea Point Lighthouse

Ke'e Beach

Haena

Kilauea

Astonishing erosion has created most spectacular coastline in Hawaii, viewable from aircraft and small boats.

Kalalau Trail

Hanalei

Anahola

Na Pali Coast

Kalalau Valley

Hanakapiai Falls

Hanalei Valley

Kokee

Alakai Swamp

Some 460 inches of rainfall annually give this peak claim to "the rainiest place on earth."

Kapaa

Barking Sands

State Park

Opaekaa Falls

Waialeale 5148 +

Wailua

Waimea Canyon

Kawaikini 5243 +

Kamokila Village

Wailua Falls

Fern Grotto

Hanamaulu

Multi-hued red rocks have given this 2000-foot deep chasm the nickname "Grand Canyon of the Pacific."

Lihue

Nawiliwili Bay

Kekaha

Waimea

Kalaheo

Koloa

Hawaii's first commercial sugar plantation and mill established here in 1835.

Fort Elizabeth

Hanapepe

Poipu

Kaulakahi Channel

In 1815 a commercial agent for the Russian government makes an abortive attempt to annex Kauai to Russian Empire, building Fort Elizabeth in the process.

Spouting Horn

Kauai Channel

Kauai

| 0 | Miles | 10 |

| 0 | Kilometers | 10 |

Oldest of Hawaii's main islands (leaving aside the hundred-odd atolls and islets stretching 1300 miles to the northwest, some of which in eons past were once themselves high-rising islands), Kauai shows the effects of its age in the most dramatic erosion forms in the State. Mt. Waialeale, the remains of the single volcano which formed the island, rises 5150 feet at its center, and is famed as the place of heaviest rainfall in the world, averaging 460 inches annually (it is the island's overall lushness which has given rise to its nickname, the Garden Island). To the northwest of Waialeale, on a 4000' plateau, lies the Alakai Swamp, nearly inaccessible, perpetually covered with mist and clouds, home to stunted trees, ferns, and mosses, as well as to a a handful of bird species now extremely rare or wholly extinct elsewhere in the State. Along the northwestern coast lie the incredible fluted cliffs of the Na Pali coast, fully visible only by aircraft or boat, or to the hiker intrepid enough to attempt the rugged Kalalau Trail zigzagging above the shoreline. Most famous of all, perhaps, is Waimea Canyon, drainage channel for the Alakai, and sometimes called the "Grand Canyon of the Pacific," an exaggeration forgivable in view of the canyon's size in relation to the whole island.

Separated from Oahu by the 75-mile-wide, two-mile deep Kauai Channel, Kauai has historically been removed from the other main islands, and is famed as the only island (together with its small dependency, Niihau) never invaded by Kamehameha I, although he did succeed in bringing the island under his dominion by treaty in 1810. Kauai seems quietly proud of this historic separateness, just as it proudly claims the mythical *menehune*, a race of "little people" who populated Hawaii before the arrival of the Polynesians and whose exploits included the "Menehune Fishpond" near Lihue, and the "Menehune Ditch" near the town of Waimea. In that same Waimea on January 20, 1778, Captain Cook first trod Hawaiian soil; some forty years later a commercial agent for the Russian government, going far beyond his commission, made an abortive attempt to place Kauai under the czarist crown, constructing a fort at the mouth of the Waimea River in the process. The stone and earthenwork remnants of Fort Elizabeth, named for the czar's wife, remain to this day.

Fourth largest of the islands, Kauai seems intent on avoiding the wholesale tourist development which has so altered portions of the three larger islands, hoping to balance "quality" resorts with the relaxed, small town atmosphere which pervades the island. (Kauai may be the one place in the world where the police force has asked local drivers to speed up, in the hope of easing some of the congestion in and out of Lihue during "rush hours.")

The sun sets behind an 'ohia tree in Kokee State Park.

(Previous page): *Taro fields dot the floor of the Hanalei Valley, perhaps the loveliest in all Hawaii.*

Bill Haraguchi's 35 acres (opposite) make him the largest taro farmer in the State. His farm is a family operation, and usually one of his sons, and often his wife, are with him in the "patches," as the flooded fields are called. "My grandfather and father, they used to farm rice here, until cheap rice from your California drove them out of the market. That's okay, though—rice farming's hard work!" From where I sat, camera in hand, it looked like taro harvesting was pretty hard work, too: constantly bent at the waist, Bill would pull the tubers one-by-one, wash off the mud, cut off the stalk and roots, check for rot, and then toss it into a nearby bucket. Later the bagged taro—an average of 18,000 pounds a week—would be sent by barge to a factory in Honolulu, where it would be made into poi. Once the mainstay (with fish) of the Hawaiian diet, poi is still a favorite among many islanders, especially those of Hawaiian ancestry. For those not raised on it, it seems to be an acquired taste.

Farther down the valley cattle graze on pasture below cloud-wreathed mountains (this page).

In surroundings much as they must have been when it was built in 1837, the Waioli Mission House (this page) *stands in pristine serenity on the edge of Hanalei village. The nearby church, Hanalei Huiia* (opposite), *the third on the site, dates from 1912.*

Sunset on the Na Pali Coast, the most dramatic shoreline in all Hawaii (opposite). The only land access to the Na Pali is via the Kalalau Trail, a punishing full-day hike starting from Ke'e Beach and ending at the Kalalau Valley. About an hour and a half into the hike an arduous side trail leads to the base of Hanakapiai Falls (this page).

Lumahai, the "picture postcard" beach near Haena on the island's north coast (opposite); sunset near Nahumaalo Point on the southern shore (this page).

The wilderness experience offered by Kokee State Park is unsurpassed in the State, and includes a breathtaking overview of the Kalalau Valley (opposite). A wall of uluhe fern lines a park roadway (this page).

(Following pages): Much of the torrential rain falling on the mountainous center of the island drains westward through an arid landscape, and over millions of years has carved Waimea Canyon.

Ni'ihau,

the last Hawaiian Island

Despite my efforts, this was as close as I got to Niihau, for the entire island is under the sole ownership of the Robinson family, which has elected to limit access to the island to its residents and their invited guests.* As a journalist, I lamented this inability to "cover" one of the main Hawaiian islands; as a person who has come to know the history of Hawaii, I could sympathize with the reason: for the population of Niihau—less than 300 people—is almost completely pure Hawaiian, and the island has become, in effect, a Hawaiian preserve, the only island in Hawaii where Hawaiian remains the basic language. If outsiders began invading this sanctuary, the future of the island as a unique remnant of Hawaiian culture might soon be in doubt. (In 1959 Niihau was Hawaii's only electoral district to vote against accepting American statehood, a measure which the territory as a whole approved by a 17 to one margin.)

The island was purchased in its entirety in 1864 from King Kamehameha V by an ancestor of the present owners, and has been operated as a cattle and sheep ranch ever since. Niihau's low profile and its position in the "rain shadow" of Kauai means the island receives little rainfall, so scrub vegetation, including *kiawe* (mesquite) for making charcoal, dominates the landscape.

Aside from its reputation as the "forbidden island," Niihau is famed for its shell leis, painstakingly strung from tiny shells unique to its beaches, and selling for prices into the hundreds and even thousands of dollars.

Subsequent to my coverage of Kauai and Niihau, Niihau Ranch began helicopter tours of the island which permit outsiders to overfly and land on the uninhabited eastern side of the island.

Oʻahu:
at the Center
of Hawaiʻi

Huge waves created by winter storms make this one of surfing's legendary shores.

Kauai Channel

North Shore

Windward Coast

Polynesian Cultural Center

Waimea
Laie

☐ Waimea Falls Park

Kaena Point

Waialua

Haleiwa

+ *Kaala 4020*

Waianae Range

Wahiawa
Schofield Barracks

Makaha
Waianae

Mililani

Nanakuli

Waipahu

Pearl City

Aiea

Pearl Harbor

Makakilo

Ewa

Ewa Beach

Waianae Coast

Barbers Point

Koolau Range

Kaneohe Bay

Mokapu Peninsula

Kaneohe

Kailua

Nuuanu Pali

Maunawili

Waimanalo

Sea Life Park ☐

Makapuu Point

Waikiki

Honolulu

Diamond Head

Koko Head

Kaiwi Channel

Oahu

Strategic value of this superb harbor drew the attention of the United States during the late 19th Century, eventually leading to annexation of Hawaii in 1898.

0 Miles   10

0 Kilometers   10

Third largest of the islands, Oahu was formed from two large volcanoes, the remnants of which today compose the Koolau Range to the east and the Waianae Mountains to the west. Oahu is home to more than 80% of Hawaii's people, a population concentration which began soon after the European discovery, for—despite the loose claims in much tourist literature that "O'ahu" translates into the island's nickname, "the Gathering Place," (no linguistic evidence supports that interpretation)—in the pre-contact era Oahu did not have a large population, and was generally subservient to Kauai and the island of Hawaii. In fact, Oahu's ascendancy stems from the days of Western contact and the need of the newcomers' square-rigged sailing ships for a protected, deep-draft harbor. The island's population has grown inexorably ever since, fed by both Neighbor Island transplants as well as newcomers to the State. Only from the 1970s has this trend toward concentration somewhat lessened, as the Neighbor Islands have slightly increased their share of the total population.

Since the great majority of the island's population is concentrated within the urban concentration thought of as Honolulu (in fact, the city's legal definition encompasses the entire island, as well as the hundred-odd minor Northwestern Hawaiian Islands stretching to Kure Atoll fourteen hundred miles away), it tends to be forgotten that much of Oahu is rural and agricultural land. Historically, Oahu has been a significant producer of sugar and pineapple within the State, but with the steady growth of the island's population and the consequent increase in land values, more and more of that land has been sought for housing and commercial development, and agricultural acreage relentlessly disappears. Today the great majority of Oahu's population is employed either in government or in the service industries, principally tourism.

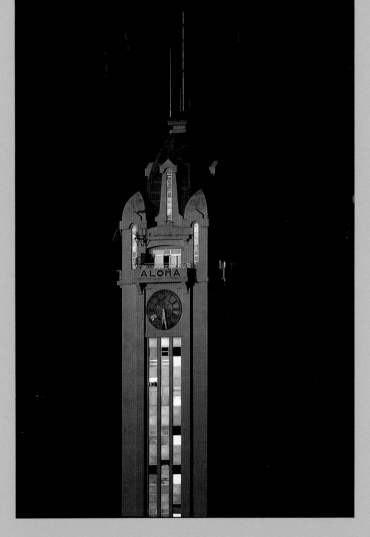

Honolulu's famed Aloha Tower, a harbor-side fixture since 1926, glistens in the late afternoon sun.

Linking the Waianae Range to the west with the Koolau Range on the east, the Central Plateau (this page) has for decades produced the bulk of Oahu's pineapple and sugar crops. But creeping urbanization, fed by a perennially tight housing market, steadily reduces the acreage available for agriculture. Framed by the Koolau Range, Windward Oahu stretches before the Nuuanu Pali (opposite).

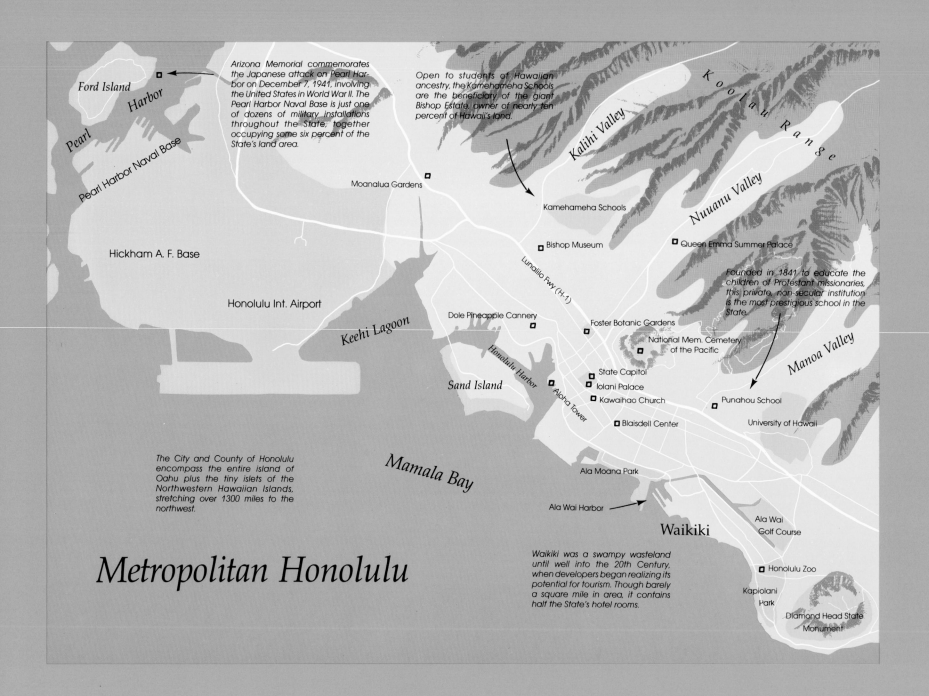

Arizona Memorial commemorates the Japanese attack on Pearl Harbor on December 7, 1941, involving the United States in World War II. The Pearl Harbor Naval Base is just one of dozens of military installations throughout the State, together occupying some six percent of the State's land area.

Open to students of Hawaiian ancestry, the Kamehameha Schools are the beneficiary of the giant Bishop Estate, owner of nearly ten percent of Hawaii's land.

Ford Island

Pearl Harbor

Koolau Range

Kalihi Valley

Nuuanu Valley

Pearl Harbor Naval Base

Moanalua Gardens

Kamehameha Schools

Bishop Museum

Queen Emma Summer Palace

Hickham A. F. Base

Lunalilo Fwy (H-1)

Founded in 1841 to educate the children of Protestant missionaries, this private, non-secular institution is the most prestigious school in the State.

Honolulu Int. Airport

Dole Pineapple Cannery

Foster Botanic Gardens

Manoa Valley

Keehi Lagoon

National Mem. Cemetery of the Pacific

Honolulu Harbor

State Capitol

Iolani Palace

Sand Island

Aloha Tower

Kawaihao Church

Punahou School

Blaisdell Center

University of Hawaii

The City and County of Honolulu encompass the entire island of Oahu plus the tiny islets of the Northwestern Hawaiian Islands, stretching over 1300 miles to the northwest.

Mamala Bay

Ala Moana Park

Ala Wai Harbor

Ala Wai Golf Course

Waikiki

Waikiki was a swampy wasteland until well into the 20th Century, when developers began realizing its potential for tourism. Though barely a square mile in area, it contains half the State's hotel rooms.

Honolulu Zoo

Metropolitan Honolulu

Kapiolani Park

Diamond Head State Monument

Honolulu took its name from, and grew up around, Honolulu Harbor—the "sheltered haven" or "protected bay" which proved indispensable to deep-draft Western vessels. Once given that impetus, Honolulu's growth fed on itself: trading center, commercial center, then, from 1845, capital of the kingdom (having been transferred from Lahaina). The use and development of Pearl Harbor as a naval installation from the last quarter of the 19th century further stimulated the city's growth. Then the city's position as the State's sea and air transportation hub ensured its primacy when tourism became big business from the 1950s onward (even today Waikiki, with a bare square mile of land, contains some 35,000 hotel rooms—half the State's total).

Bounded *ewa* (on the west) by Pearl Harbor and

Diamond Head (on the east) by Diamond Head itself, Metropolitan Honolulu occupies a narrow coastal strip between the Koolau Range *mauka* (inland) and the Pacific Ocean *makai* (seaward). Cities within a city, from Pearl Harbor to Keehi Lagoon is dominated by military installations; from Keehi to Downtown is found much of the city's industrial plant; Downtown encompasses corporate, banking, and governmental headquarters, as well as Chinatown and most of historical Honolulu; Downtown to Waikiki, commercial and light industry predominate; tourism and recreation facilities characterize the area from Waikiki to Diamond Head. Inland, residential areas predominate and stretch *mauka* up valleys and along ridges descending from the Koolaus.

The city from the top of Diamond Head at dusk.

*As recently as 1960, Aloha Tower was Honolulu's tallest building.
Statehood, rapid population increase and a booming tourist sector brought
three decades of economic growth which have transformed the city's
downtown area almost beyond recognition: Bishop Square* (opposite) *and
downtown viewed from Aloha Tower* (this page).

Honolulu grew up around its harbor, and nearly all the State's imports still pass first through its container port (opposite), and are then transshipped to the neighbor islands as necessary. Honolulu's rapid growth has produced problems familiar to most large cities, including rush-hour traffic jams on its single, cross-town freeway.

Blessed by a superb location and climate, Honolulu is one of America's most attractive and livable cities. An outrigger canoe crew works out on the Ala Wai Canal bordering Waikiki (this page). Just ewa of Waikiki the Ala Wai Yacht Harbor is minutes from anywhere in the city (opposite).

Traditional and modern in Waikiki architecture: the famous facade of the Royal Hawaiian Hotel facing Waikiki Beach (opposite), and, the stark lines of the Waikiki Seiwa building (this page).

Where it's at: Waikiki Beach in full swing (opposite). *Dean of Waikiki's beachboys, pure Hawaiian "Steamboat" Mokuahi* (this page) *has been a fixture on the beach for over 50 years.*

Reminders of Hawaii's missionary past: Punahou School (this page), today the most prestigious private school in the State, dates from 1841, when it was founded to educate the children of the Protestant missionaries. (The school has long been non-denominational and open to the general population.) Kawaiahao Church (opposite) built in 1842, conducts services in both English and Hawaiian.

The years of contract labor immigration from China and Japan brought to Hawaii thousands of adherents to Oriental faiths. Two of Oahu's most famous Buddhist temples are the Kuan Yin Temple near downtown Honolulu (this page), *which primarily serves the Chinese population, and the Byodo-In Temple on Windward Oahu* (opposite), *a modern re-creation of the original in Kyoto, Japan which dates from the 11th Century .*

Moloka'i and Lāna'i: Yesterday's Hawai'i

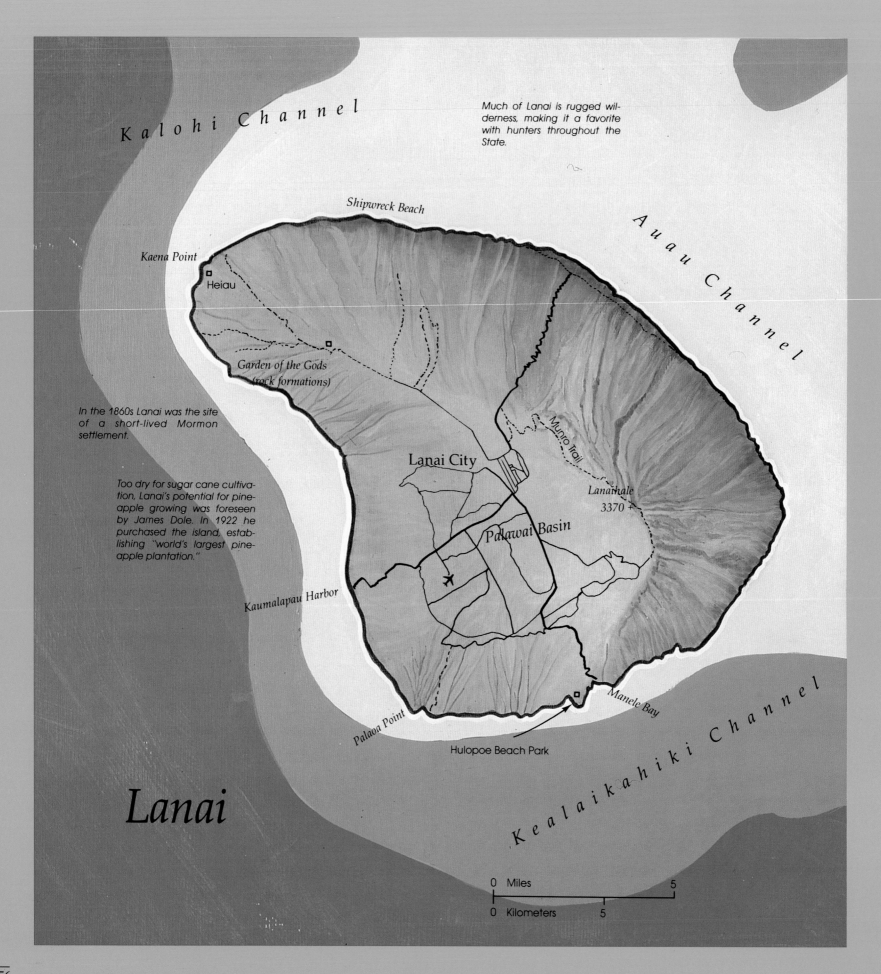

Kalohi Channel

Much of Lanai is rugged wilderness, making it a favorite with hunters throughout the State.

Shipwreck Beach

Auau Channel

Kaena Point

Heiau

Garden of the Gods
(rock formations)

In the 1860s Lanai was the site of a short-lived Mormon settlement.

Munro Trail

Lanai City

Too dry for sugar cane cultivation, Lanai's potential for pineapple growing was foreseen by James Dole. In 1922 he purchased the island, establishing "world's largest pineapple plantation."

Lanaihale
3370 +

Palawai Basin

Kaumalapau Harbor

Manele Bay

Palaoa Point

Hulopoe Beach Park

Kealaikahiki Channel

Lanai

0   Miles   5

0   Kilometers   5

Lāna'i, the Pineapple Island

While rapid development has swept over much of Hawaii in the thirty years since statehood, two islands have been relatively untouched—until now—by this tide.

Few would dispute the aptness of the nickname applied to Lanai, the smaller of the two: the "Pineapple Isle." Purchased in 1922 in nearly its entirety by the pioneer of the Hawaiian pineapple industry, James Dole, Lanai has for the last half-century been essentially a giant pineapple plantation. Virtually the entire working population of the island is, or once was, employed by the Dole Corporation (since 1961 a subsidiary of Castle & Cooke) in farming some 13,000 acres of "pines," as the fruit is called. Although sometimes billed as "the world's largest pineapple plantation," less than a quarter of the island is suited to cultivation, much of the remainder being rugged terrain, hiding wild sheep, turkey, and deer.

Traveling to Lanai was a bit of an experience in itself: from the moment I boarded the commuter plane at Honolulu airport for the early morning flight to the island, I knew Lanai was going to be unlike any other Hawaiian island. And so it would prove to be: for everyone else on the plane seemed to know each other, joking and chatting about their visit to the big city. The Lanai Airport would reinforce the feeling: no taxi, no pay telephone (the airline's telephone was sitting on the counter when I walked up, ready for such situations), no hotel pick-up. So I hitched a ride in the jeep of some accommodating construction workers.

Lanai, in short, was the quintessential friendly small town. The presence of the construction workers, however, was an indication that Lanai was nearing the end of an era, for they were on the island working on the construction of two large new tourist hotels (to supplement the 10-room Hotel Lanai, built in 1927 and for decades the only visitor accommodation). Thus Lanai, up to now on the itinerary only of hunters, journalists, and the rare intrepid tourist, is soon to have a taste of the tourism the other islands have known for years. The push to diversify the island into tourism has the support of most of the population, who see a tourist industry as a chance for their children and themselves to remain on Lanai. Those like myself who had the chance to know Lanai "before," will hope that tourism comes without destroying the warmth of the people that made Lanai the friendliest place I visited in Hawaii.

Four-year-old Rex Calderon waits outside his day-care center in Lanai City.

Long known for the pineapple fields rising through the iron-oxide-rich soil of the Palawai Basin (opposite), Lanaians expect the "Lanai Plan" to add tourism to their economic future. Sunset highlights the island's famed Norfolk Island Pines (this page).

Pausing in one of the most arduous—and highly-paid—jobs on the Dole plantation, Florencia Villamor (this page) plants pineapple "crowns" by plunging them through holes in a polyethylene strip. Some 20 months later each plant's single fruit will approach its ideal weight of 3-5 pounds, and a picking crew will follow the 65' boom of a "parasite" harvester through the fields (opposite). Placed on a conveyer belt, the fruit is carried to a bin on the truck. Once the bin is full, the harvester raises itself off the truck bed on hydraulic jacks (hence the term "parasite"), and truck and fruit will head for the island's Kaumalapau Harbor, where a waiting barge will haul the "pines" to Dole's Honolulu cannery. Although it is the world's highest-cost producer, Hawaii is able to compete against foreign growers with a combination of consistent quality and rapid delivery to the U.S. market.

Lanai City appears the quintessential plantation town, and most of its houses (opposite) were built to a pattern which changed but little over the decades. Often under clouds hanging over the ridge to the east, the town's 1500' elevation and pine trees belie its tropical location. Like most of Lanai's 3000-odd residents, Josephine Allas (standing in front of her home, this page) wouldn't live anywhere else, and the love Lanai's residents express for their town and island calls into question the usual reputation of the "company town."

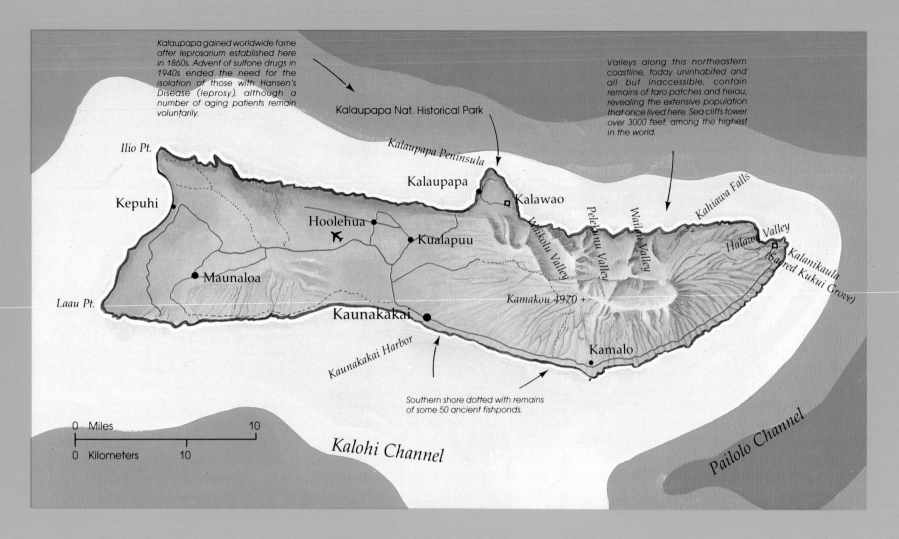

Kalaupapa gained worldwide fame after leprosarium established here in 1860s. Advent of sulfone drugs in 1940s ended the need for the isolation of those with Hansen's Disease (leprosy), although a number of aging patients remain voluntarily.

Valleys along this northeastern coastline, today uninhabited and all but inaccessible, contain remains of taro patches and heiau, revealing the extensive population that once lived here. Sea cliffs tower over 3000 feet, among the highest in the world.

Kalaupapa Nat. Historical Park

Kalaupapa Peninsula

Ilio Pt.

Kepuhi

Kalaupapa

Kalawao

Hoolehua

Kualapuu

Waikolu Valley

Pelekunu Valley

Wailau Valley

Kahiawa Falls

Halawa Valley

Kalanikaula (Sacred Kukui Grove)

Maunaloa

Laau Pt.

Kamakou 4970 +

Kaunakakai

Kamalo

Kaunakakai Harbor

Southern shore dotted with remains of some 50 ancient fishponds.

0 Miles 10

0 Kilometers 10

Kalohi Channel

Pailolo Channel

Moloka'i, the Friendly Isle

Fifth largest of the islands, Molokai's 261 square miles were shaped into a very rough rectangle 38 miles long and about 10 wide by two volcanoes; considerably later in geologic time a third, much smaller volcano erupted against the northern side of the island to form the Kalaupapa ("flat plain") Peninsula. (In the late 19th Century this peninsula would gain worldwide fame as the site of Hawaii's leprosarium.) Heavy precipitation falling on the eastern end of the island has carved spectacular valleys from the three-thousand-foot sea cliffs which line the northern (windward) shore. In these valleys the scattered remains of *heiau* and taro patch terraces are reminders of the people who inhabited them long ago; today they are deserted, virtually inaccessible except by helicopter or boat. Only an aerial perspective does justice to this part of the island, and flying that coastline after a heavy rain brings the reward of leaping, feathery waterfalls plunging to the sea—one of which, Kahiwa (1750')—is the highest in the State. Across the spine of mountains, lining the southern shore, the remains of more than 50 fishponds are perhaps the most vivid and best preserved reminders of ancient Hawaii's development.

As with Lanai, pineapple has been a part of Molokai's past, and the island has been for the most part bypassed by tourist development. But unlike its smaller neighbor, and to a degree unique in Hawaii, Molokai's people have aggressively opposed such development, ardent in their desire to retain the "old Hawaii" rural character of their island. (Close to forty percent of Molokai's 6500 residents are of Hawaiian ancestry—Niihau aside, the highest percentage in the State.)

The efforts to "keep Molokai Molokai" have largely succeeded; many of the island's visitors are residents of the neighbor islands, seeking a respite from their more harried existence. (Many Honolulu residents declare the island their favorite, since it encapsulates the Hawaii of their past, a Hawaii in danger of disappearing on the other neighbor islands, and long since departed from Honolulu.) But the opposition to tourism has come at a high price: with the demise of the pineapple industry in the 1980s, Molokai has been left with few employment sources beside cattle ranching and truck farming. For the moment, it appears that the island's long history of high unemployment is likely to continue.

Kupeke fishpond is but one of some fifty on Molokai's south shore built in ancient times.

Skeletal against evening's fading light, the hardy kiawe *(opposite,* known on the mainland as the mesquite) is so widespread in the island's drier regions that it is hard to imagine them without it. And yet the kiawe is not native to the islands, and was not even introduced until 1828, when a French Catholic priest planted seeds brought from a botanical garden in Paris. Most of low-rising Western Molokai is hay fields and cattle rangeland of Molokai Ranch, the island's largest private landowner (this page).*

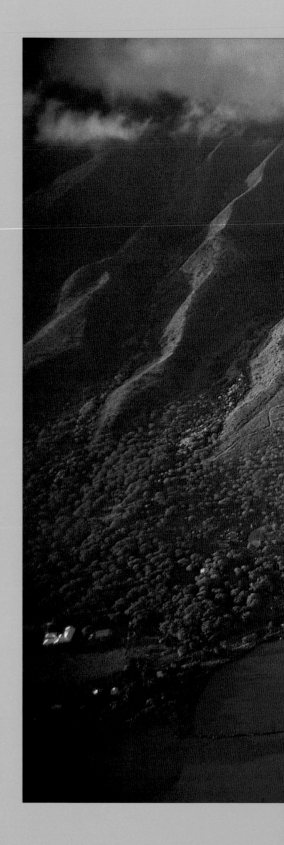

The Halawa Valley (this page), *thought to be one of the oldest inhabited sites in Hawaii, was until recently home to a large population of taro farmers, until reduced demand and the threat of tsunami (tidal waves) drove them out. The rugged volcanic slopes of eastern Molokai rise to nearly 5000', catching most of the island's rain (opposite). Seen here from the drier southern side, the mountains hide valleys opening onto Molokai's northern shore; considered nearly inaccessible today, in centuries past they were home to much of the island's population.*

Kalaupapa:

a Special Place,

a Special Story

Eons ago, long after the two volcanoes which formed the main body of Molokai had ceased their activity, and millennia of trade winds had swept in from the sea, dropping their moisture to carve the awesome cliffs rising vertically from the island's north shore, another, much smaller volcano bubbled up through the sea's surface, spreading its flow of lava against the cliff, creating a small, flat peninsula. Thus by an accident of geology was this peninsula born, cut off physically from the main of Molokai, almost as though it were a separate island. More millennia would pass, and men would discover and settle these islands. Then centuries more would pass, and another accident of nature and a decision of man would complete the isolation geology had begun, separating the peninsula totally from the rest of the island overlooking it.

I went to Kalaupapa knowing the rudiments of its history: of how, in the mid-19th Century, leprosy— dreaded, disfiguring, incurable leprosy—had begun to spread through the population of Hawaii; of how, in 1865, the Hawaiian government, desperate for a solution, had decided to isolate those with leprosy on the Kalaupapa peninsula; and how, in January of 1866, the first of many "shipments" was left at Kalawao, on the peninsula's windswept eastern shore.

The conditions these early arrivals met were primitive, at times anarchical, for if the authorities' planning had been minimal, their provision of supervision, facilities, and medical care was almost nonexistent. Knowing that they would never return to the "outside," in many instances disowned by family and friends, and with the knowledge that in any case they faced a slow, perhaps painful, death, many of those abandoned to Kalaupapa lost their moral bearings.

For the others, it was a matter of relying on each other to make the best of it. And so two days before Christmas of that first year on Kalaupapa, a small group of men and women came together to form the Siloama Church; five years later, in 1871, they would complete the simple wooden structure. In it—for the building still stands (**opposite page**)—is a simple wooden plaque whose words evoke the conditions those early outcasts faced:

Thrust out by mankind, these 12 women and 23 men crying aloud to God their only refuge formed a church the first in the desolation that was Kalawao.

I went knowing, too, of the the outlines of the story of Father Damien de Veuster, the Belgian priest who had come to Hawaii in 1864, working first in parishes on Oahu and the Big Island for nine years. Then in 1873 Damien was assigned to Molokai, and began the work on Kalaupapa that was to make his name known around the world. Over a period of sixteen years, heedless of the danger to his own health, Damien would use his varied talents—as pastor, carpenter, persuader—in tireless pursuit of improving the physical and spiritual conditions at Kalawao. Even beyond his own efforts, his example would inspire others to dedicate their lives or money to his cause; prompted by his appeals, the Hawaiian government slowly improved medical facilities and living conditions for the Kalaupapa patients. Then in 1885 Damien himself contracted the disease, and four years later, at age 49, died at Kalawao.

That, very briefly, is the awe-inspiring story of Father Damien and his life of sacrifice for the outcasts of Kalaupapa. But there is another aspect to the story

A statue of Father Damien stands alongside St. Joseph's Church, the second of two churches he built on "topside" Molokai (this page). Damien's work on Kalaupapa helped focus worldwide attention on the conditions at the leprosarium, and led to the eventual construction of medical facilities and adequate housing at Kalawao on the peninsula's eastern shore (opposite), original site of the settlement.

*Many of Kalaupapa's patients appear years younger than their true ages:
Kenso Seki has been a Kalaupapa resident for all but 18 of his 78 years.
Most afternoons find him in his workshop (this page), where he makes
and gives away, among other small items, his "Kalaupapa Can Opener"
which aid deformed fingers in pulling the tab from beverage cans. Mildred
Nakanishi, a native of the Big Island, came to Kalaupapa in 1942, when
she was 38 years old. Though her mind remains bright, she is now con-
fined to the settlement's hospital. She poses (opposite) with an old friend,
Sister Wilma, the hospital's head of nursing, whom Mildred assisted as a
nurse's aide in her early years at Kalaupapa.*

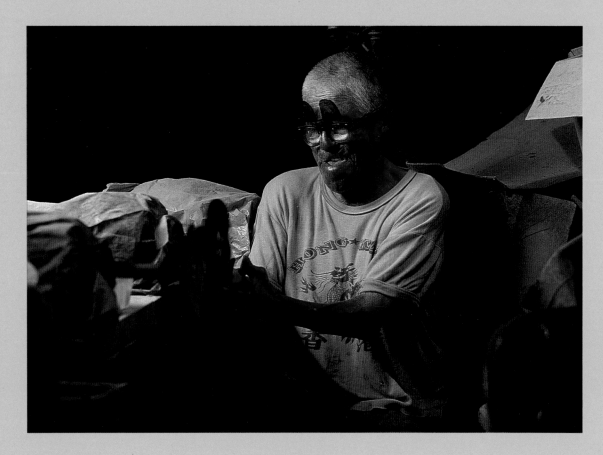

of Damien and Hawaii which to me is equally wonderful. In front of the Capitol in Honolulu stands a statue; often draped with leis, it is not a statue to a military hero, nor a politician, nor a king from Hawaii's past. It is a statue of Father Damien, a simple priest from Belgium who devoted his life to some people of Hawaii. No statue anywhere has ever done more honor to the people who erected it.

So I had gone to Kalaupapa knowing something of its history, of the awful conditions of its early years, of Father Damien's sacrifice, and thinking that my journey would bring that tragic history alive. But in the days of my visit I discovered instead the Kalaupapa of today—that for the aging patients who have elected to remain, the hellish Kalaupapa of the history books is no more; that for them it had become their chosen home. For with the development of sulfone-drug treatment in the 1940s, the scourge of leprosy—or Hansen's Disease, as it has come to be known, named for the Norwegian discoverer of its bacillus—had at last been conquered; under treatment, patients ceased to be contagious. With new cases being treated on an outpatient basis, new admissions to the colony ended in 1969; even before, patients with arrested cases had been free to travel off the peninsula.

As my stay at Kalaupapa drew to a close, I joined the "regulars" one last time at Rea's Bar, the settlement's afternoon "social club" and posed a question: Was there bitterness at having been so cruelly selected by fate, then cast out by society? Nicki Ramos, who, like most of the others, has been at Kalaupapa nearly all his adult life, responded: "Bitterness? I think there was, at first. But you have to take life as it comes—it's no good to stay angry about it. Just hurts you twice. And after a while you began to see that Kalaupapa was a blessing in disguise, because it meant being able to live as normal human beings, not freaks like we would have been on the outside. For us, Kalaupapa has been a haven."

Declared a National Historical Park in 1980, Kalaupapa is today jointly administered by the National Park Service and the Hawaii State Department of Health. Supervised day tours, arriving by mule or small plane, are available to any visitors 16 or over willing to respect the colony's privacy; each year thousands make the trip from "topside" Molokai. But with a median patient age near 70, Kalaupapa's days as an active settlement are nearing an end, and the question of its future increasingly arises. The hope of many is that the peninsula will remain a park forever—both as a reminder of its past and a tranquil wilderness haven in a changing world.

Maui:
the Variety of
the Valley Isle

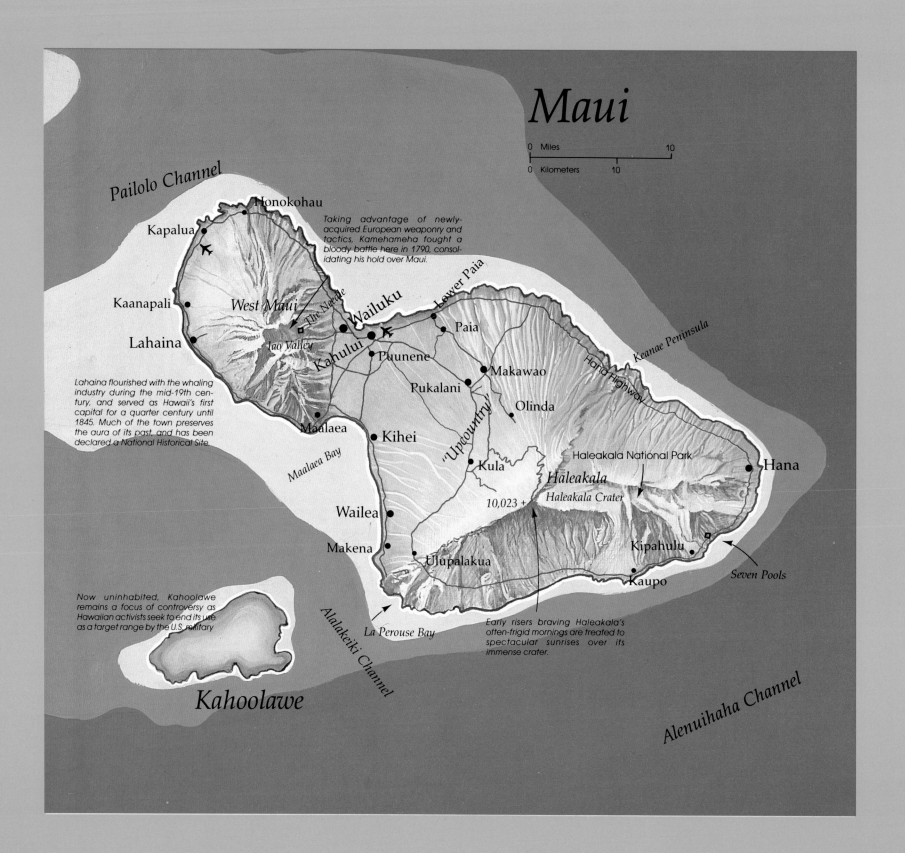

Maui

0 Miles 10

0 Kilometers 10

Pailolo Channel

Honokohau

Kapalua

Kaanapali

West Maui

The Needle

Wailuku

Lower Paia

Paia

Taking advantage of newly-acquired European weaponry and tactics, Kamehameha fought a bloody battle here in 1790, consolidating his hold over Maui.

Lahaina

Kahului

Iao Valley

Puunene

Makawao

Pukalani

Keanae Peninsula

Hana Highway

Lahaina flourished with the whaling industry during the mid-19th century, and served as Hawaii's first capital for a quarter century until 1845. Much of the town preserves the aura of its past, and has been declared a National Historical Site.

Maalaea

Kihei

"Upcountry"

Olinda

Maalaea Bay

Haleakala National Park

Kula

Haleakala

Haleakala Crater

10,023 +

Wailea

Now uninhabited, Kahoolawe remains a focus of controversy as Hawaiian activists seek to end its use as a target range by the U.S. military.

Makena

Kipahulu

Ulupalakua

Seven Pools

La Perouse Bay

Kaupo

Early risers braving Haleakala's often-frigid mornings are treated to spectacular sunrises over its immense crater.

Alalakeiki Channel

Kahoolawe

Alenuihaha Channel

Maui no ka 'oi, Mauians like to say of their favorite island: Maui is the best. It is easy to see their point, for Maui has it all : history, beaches, watersports, the chill evenings of the upcountry, protea nurseries, spectacular scenery, rugged terrain, the quiet life of the "valley" towns, and the excitement of Lahaina and the Kaanapali Coast resorts.

Second largest of the chain, Maui was formed when lava flows from two volcanoes joined at their bases, creating the isthmus, or valley, which inspires the island's nickname. Across that isthmus, rich with sugar cane and pineapple fields, the trade winds sweeping in from the ocean are funneled into the famous Maui "breezes" (usually more akin to winds) which moderate its temperature and create some of the best windsurfing conditions in the world. On the western side of the isthmus the West Maui Mountains are the heavily eroded remains of the older volcano, while East Maui is formed by the younger volcano, 10,000-foot Haleakala, meaning "House of the Sun." Here, according to legend, the demigod Maui—the source of the island's name—lassoed the sun, slowing its path across the sky so that his mother's kapa would have time to dry. (Another Hawaiian legend holds that it was this same Maui who raised up the islands when his fishhook caught in the ocean floor.)

In a less remote era, historic Maui centered around Lahaina, which grew to prominence after 1819, when the whaling ships began making it their port of call. For a quarter century thereafter Lahaina was the capital of the kingdom, until Honolulu's growing importance led Kamehameha III to transfer the capital there in 1845. Today most of Maui's population lives on the isthmus, whether at the twin towns of Kahului and Wailuku (the major commercial and administrative centers of the island), on the paniolo-oriented "upcountry" slopes of Haleakala, or in the new communities of the Kihei area.

It is at Lahaina, too, that the island's tourist industry is focused, with enormous resort development northward along the Kaanapali Coast. Maui's tourism is second only to Oahu's, and growing at a rapid pace, having long since surpassed sugar and pineapple as the island's most important economic sector. Paradoxically, Maui's tourism, while still only a fraction of Oahu's, is much more visible, since in Oahu's case tourists tend to be concentrated in the confines of Waikiki and lost in the mass of the resident population. It is this visibility, together with the island's attractiveness to mainland transplants, which lead many of Maui's *kamaainas* to lament the changes and population growth which have swept the island in the past two decades. "We're getting to be just like Oahu," an acquaintance complained. While the comparison is an exaggeration, the concern is understandable, for Maui today has a highly attractive balance of development, quiet pace, and economic opportunity.

Hawaii's State Bird, the nene, on the slopes of Haleakala

The massive bulk of Haleakala looms over Maui's isthmus like a mountain deserving of the name "House of the Sun." A drive to the 10,000' summit for sunrise over the immense crater can bring a spectacular visual reward (opposite). Bundled against bitter cold, early-risers greet the dawn at the crater rim (this page).

The summit and crater of Haleakala are home to the rare silversword (opposite), found only in the severe conditions at the tops of Hawaii's highest peaks (the plant is also found at the summits of the Big Island's Mauna Kea and Mauna Loa). Though resembling in shape the yucca of the American southwest, the silversword is actually a member of the sunflower family and related to the daisy. The plant may take from four to twenty years to mature, then sends up a single, summer-blooming flower stalk, and dies. Haleakala's lower slopes provide ideal conditions for the protea (PRO-tee-uh; this page), which has become a significant Maui export.

*On the lower slopes of Haleakala is found Maui's famed "upcountry"—
rolling pasture sprinkled with eucalyptus, where a pair of large cattle
ranches, the Haleakala and the Ulupalakua (pictured, opposite) run most
of the stock. Some 6500 head are fattened on the Ulupalakua's 30,000 acres,
and, while cattle are usually treated in a modern squeeze chute, two or three
times a year the ranch's paniolos hold an old-fashioned roundup, roping
and wrestling the young calves to the ground (this page). "We like to keep
our skills up," the ranch manager, Ed Rice, commented. "And besides," he
said with a grin, "it's a lot more fun."*

"Heavenly Hana" they call it, a verdant oasis laced with cascading water (such as Wailua Falls, opposite) at Maui's extreme eastern tip. But for her residents, Hana is as much a state of mind as a place, and the tortuous, cliff-hugging Hana Highway (three hours, and 56 narrow bridges; this page) is no hardship, for it has protected Hana from the development that has altered so much of Maui in the last two decades.

Marvel of erosion, the "Needle" stands in the Iao Valley of the West Maui Mountains (opposite). Every day a flotilla of snorkel boats descends on tiny Molokini (this page), three miles off Makena Point, its crater shape a reminder of the extinct volcano lying below.

Sunset silhouettes a row of palms at Kapalua on West Maui
(opposite). *Kamaole Beach, near Kihei, is one of the finest beaches
on the island's southwest coast* (this page).

West Maui's Kaanapali Coast (opposite) was the first area of the Neighbor Islands to undergo extensive tourism development. History-laden Lahaina is the hub of West Maui and was Hawaii's capital from 1820 to 1845. Despite having become thoroughly tourist-oriented, much of Lahaina's development maintains an architectural style evocative of the 19th Century, and the town was declared a National Historic District in 1962. The Baldwin Home (this page), today a museum, dates from the mid-1830s, and served as residence and dispensary for the missionary doctor Dwight Baldwin and his family until 1868.

PIONEER INN
HOUSE RULES

You must pay you rent in advance.

You must not let you room go one day back.

Women is not allow in you room.

If you wet or burn you bed you going out.

You are not allow to gambel in you room.

You are not allow to give you bed to you freand.

If you freand stay overnight you must see the mgr.

You must leave you room at 11 am so the women can clean you room.

Only on Sunday you can sleep all day.

You are not allow in the down stears in the seating room or in the dinering room or in the kitchen when you are drunk.

You are not allow to drink on the front porch.

You must use a shirt when you come to the seating room.

If you cant keep this rules please dont take the room.

Lahaina, Maui—Hawaiian Islands

Although suggestive of its whaling era, Lahaina's most famous landmark, the Pioneer Inn, was not built until 1901, some thirty years after whaling had faded from the Hawaiian scene. The original house rules continue to remind guests of the standards of civilized conduct (these pages).

The Pacific whaling fleet "made" Lahaina when it began using the town as a principal rest and refitting port from the early 1820s; four decades later the discovery of petroleum in Pennsylvania and the outbreak of the American Civil War brought the whaling era in the Pacific to a close. By an ironic turn of history, however, whales and the whaling era remain a part of Maui today. To pass the time, the crewmen of the whale ships took to scrimshaw—carving designs into whale tooth. Today Lahaina is a center for modern scrimshaw artists working in fossil ivory, primarily walrus tusk (this page). And the modern tourist can still go whale-hunting— albeit with a camera. Each November the island awaits the return of humpback whales (opposite) from their summer grounds in the waters off Alaska. The whales spend the winter months in the waters around Maui, Lanai, and the Big Island, and then after the females have calved, the humpbacks make the return journey.

Not until 1832 would the missionaries establish a station at Wailuku; that same year they founded Kaahumanu Church (the present church building, opposite, the third on the site, dates from 1876), naming it for one of Kamehameha's widows, an early Christian convert who championed the missionary cause. North of Lahaina a giant bronze Buddha on the Jodo Mission grounds commemorates the arrival of Hawaii's first Japanese immigrant workers in 1868 (this page).

Hawai'i: the "Big Island" of Hawai'i

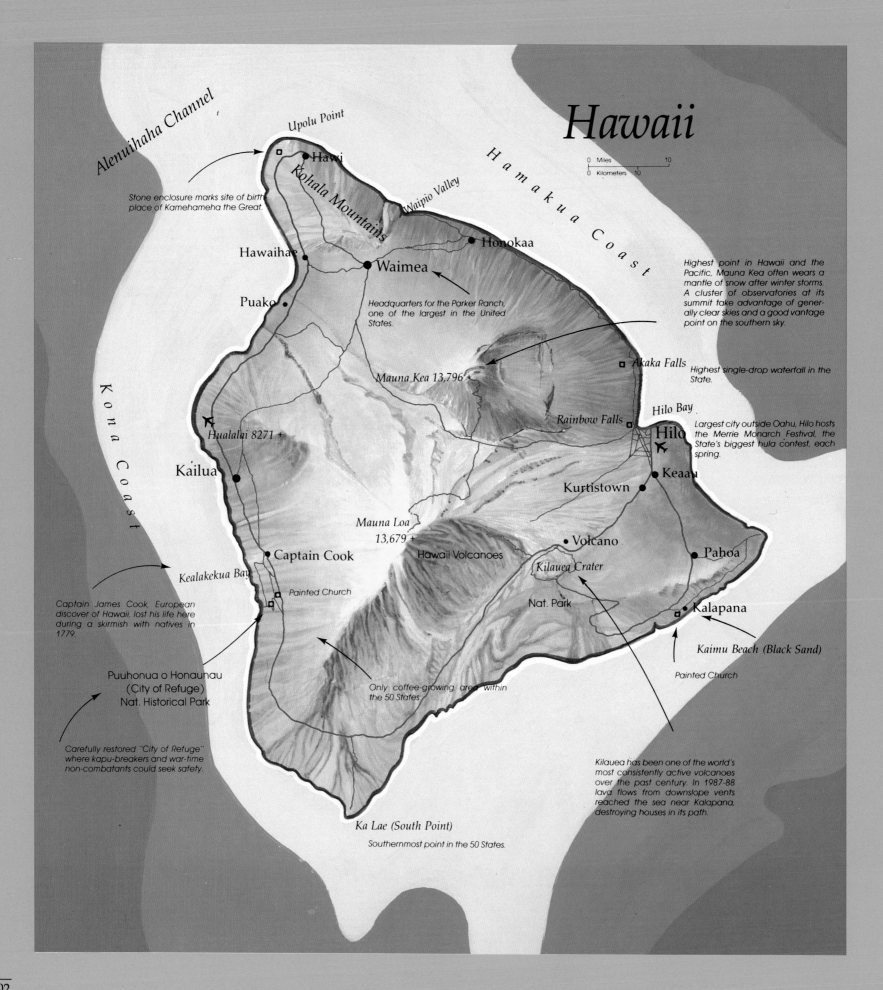

Hawaii

Alenuihaha Channel

Upolu Point

Stone enclosure marks site of birth place of Kamehameha the Great.

Hawi

Kohala Mountains

Waipio Valley

Hamakua Coast

Honokaa

Hawaihae

Waimea

Headquarters for the Parker Ranch, one of the largest in the United States.

Puako

Highest point in Hawaii and the Pacific, Mauna Kea often wears a mantle of snow after winter storms. A cluster of observatories at its summit take advantage of generally clear skies and a good vantage point on the southern sky.

Mauna Kea 13,796 +

Akaka Falls

Highest single-drop waterfall in the State.

Kona Coast

Hualalai 8271 +

Rainbow Falls

Hilo Bay

Hilo

Largest city outside Oahu, Hilo hosts the Merrie Monarch Festival, the State's biggest hula contest, each spring.

Kailua

Keaau

Kurtistown

Mauna Loa 13,679 +

Volcano

Pahoa

Hawaii Volcanoes

Kilauea Crater

Captain Cook

Kealakekua Bay

Painted Church

Nat. Park

Kalapana

Captain James Cook, European discover of Hawaii, lost his life here during a skirmish with natives in 1779.

Kaimu Beach (Black Sand)

Painted Church

Puuhonua o Honaunau (City of Refuge) Nat. Historical Park

Only coffee-growing area within the 50 States.

Carefully restored "City of Refuge" where kapu-breakers and war-time non-combatants could seek safety.

Kilauea has been one of the world's most consistently active volcanoes over the past century. In 1987-88 lava flows from downslope vents reached the sea near Kalapana, destroying houses in its path.

Ka Lae (South Point)

Southernmost point in the 50 States.

Hawaii. The "Big Island," they call it, for when Kamehameha of Hawaii conquered its neighbors and added them to his realm, the name of his island kingdom became the name for the entire chain—creating a semantic complication for all time to come.

Relative giant among its neighbors, the area of the island of Hawaii is over five times that of Maui, the next in size. Formed from five volcanoes (Mauna Kea, Kohala, Hualalai, Mauna Loa and Kilauea—the last two of which are classified as "active"), the island's 4038 square miles constitute nearly two thirds of the land area of the entire State. (To keep things in perspective, however, the Big Island is slightly smaller than the State of Connecticut.) Because of the time and distance separating one area from another (many residents of Hilo are more likely to make a trip to Honolulu than to Kona), one begins to think of the Big Island as two or three separate islands, rather than one.

Hilo, the county seat and the State's largest city outside Oahu, is the focal point for one of those "islands." Dominated by the deceptive immensity of Mauna Loa and sometimes-snowcapped Mauna Kea, the region stretches from the Hamakua Coast in the north to the southern tip of the island, Ka Lae ("South Point"—and also the southernmost point in the 50 States). Historically, this has been sugar country, and the population reflects the decades of Japanese and Filipino immigration which provided the labor force for the plantations and sugar factories. Now, as elsewhere in the State, sugar is in decline, and although Hilo retains the conservative tone of its agricultural past, the work force turns to tourism, service industries, and diversified agriculture (principally macadamia nuts and flower growing).

Two hours away, on the island's western side, the "Kona Coast," exists another "island," based on Hawaii's growth industry of the past three decades, tourism. In the rain shadow of the Big Island's volcanoes, streaked by old lava flows, much of the Kona Coast presents an arid, desolate aspect, and until the recent past had very little population, but an abundance of clear skies, barren land, and isolated, pristine beaches. These conditions were of course ideal for the tourist industry, and over the past twenty years this coast has seen large resort hotels, condominiums, and golf courses spring up one after another. With this boom has come a large influx of population, much of it from the mainland.

The Big Island contains other, lesser "islands" within its mass as well: South Kona's coffee country on the lower slopes of Mauna Loa; the cattle country with its spiritual heart in Waimea (though too scattered about the island to have a single

geographical center); the quiet rural beauty of Kohala, birthplace of Kamehameha, with its famed flat-bottomed valleys—Waipio, Waimanu and Pololu—where many of the island's early inhabitants lived. Then there are the "islands" of Hawaii's volcanoes, too inhospitable for anyone to permanently live: the summits of Mauna Loa and Mauna Kea, both over two and a half miles high, the latter with its cluster of astronomical observatories. Most inhospitable of all, Kilauea's very active caldera and vents spew fumes and molten lava down the island's southeastern flank, destroying all in its path, and sometimes reaching the sea, adding to the island. Destructive though it may be, Kilauea provides a rare opportunity to experience the process that created the islands.

For spectacular waterfalls the Big Island's Hamakua Coast is unmatched in the islands: Akaka (this page), at 442' has the highest sheer drop, while Rainbow Falls (previous page) in Hilo has the greatest annual discharge.

The heavy rainfall on the island's windward side has carved the deep
valleys and sheer cliffs of the Hamakua Coast (opposite). The flat-bottomed
valleys of the older Kohala Mountains—Pololu, Waimanu, and famed
Waipio (this page), all heavily-populated in centuries past—are evidence of
a lower sea level during the Ice Ages.

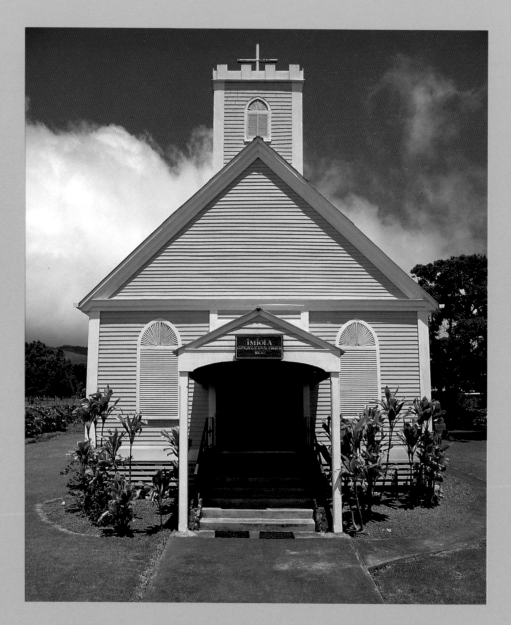

Missionary legend Lorenzo Lyons arrived in Waimea in 1832, and served there until his death 54 years later, having authored and translated hundreds of hymns for the Hawaiian people. In 1855 he and his congregation built Imiola Church (this page). An old mansion on the outskirts of Hilo (opposite) dates from the era when sugar was king.

King Sugar is dying the same slow death on Hawaii as it is elsewhere in the State, and the farmers in the Hilo area have turned to diversified agriculture also—principally macadamia nuts and flower growing. At Dan Hata's nursery in Kurtistown Raymie Padilla sorts anthuriums by size (this page). In the drier Puna area to the south scores of orchid growers have developed an export industry large enough to give the island a second nickname, "the Orchid Isle." On the opposite page, clockwise from top left, are four varieties: mid-Florida cattleya, phalaenopsid, cymbidium, and miniature cymbidium.

Perched atop the 3000' saddle joining the wet Hamakua Coast to the dry Kona side, Waimea is at the heart of the island's cattle country (this page), and is headquarters for the Parker Ranch—at 250,000 acres, one of the world's largest. The annual Parker Ranch Rodeo (opposite) has become a must event for the island's professional and amateur paniolos *(cowboys).*

In search of the outer edges of space and time, the 144-inch telescope of the Canada-France-Hawaii observatory (opposite) reads the night sky from Mauna Kea, Hawaii's highest point. The summit's cluster of eight observatories offer the world's astronomers clear, cloud-free air, remoteness from the "night shine" of big cities, and a good vantage point on the southern sky. (The Keck Observatory, scheduled for completion in 1991, will boast a segmented mirror equivalent to a 33-foot reflector, largest in the world.) A computer-generated "false-color" image captured by Ircam, an infrared camera invented at the adjacent United Kingdom Infrared Telescope reveals a pair of galaxies colliding (this page). [Ircam image: courtesy of Dr. Ian McLean, United Kingdom-Canada-Netherlands Joint Astronomy Centre]

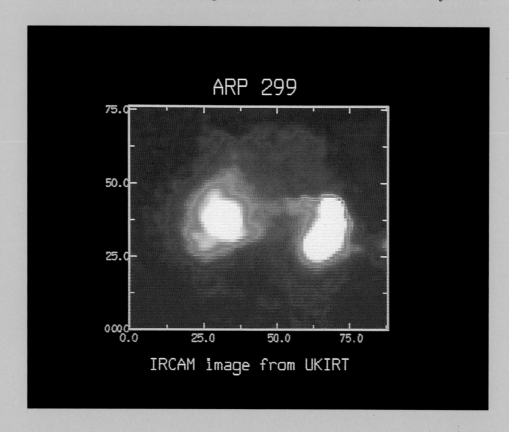

In the arid lee of the island's mountainous spine, South Kohala was little more than lava wasteland two decades ago; then the tourism industry began capitalizing on the allure of its near-constant sunshine, pristine beaches and cheap land. A string of large luxury resorts now lines the coast (opposite), with more under construction. Further south, Kailua was a favorite with Hawaiian royalty from the days of Kamehameha the Great. The Hulihee Palace (this page), dating from 1838, was used by King Kalakaua as a summer residence during the 1880s. (Across the street from Hulihee stands the oldest church building in the islands, Mokuaikaua, built of stone by the missionaries in 1837.)

Youngest of the islands, Hawaii's volcanic origins are undisguised by time: the black sand of Kaimu Beach in the Puna District resulted when flowing lava hit sea water, exploding into sand-sized granules (this page). In Hawaii Volcanoes National Park tree trunks bleach in the sun atop a recent lava flow (opposite), saved from total consumption when the red-hot lava quickly cooled as it came in contact with the tree's moist bark.

*Story without end, ongoing saga of
Hawaii's creation, Pele and ocean
meet again as a river of lava
from Kilauea's 1988 eruption
reaches the sea near Kalapana.*

Notes

1. On the photography: Anyone familiar with the photographic "literature" of Hawaii will know that there is very little original coverage in this book. The islands have been so heavily photographed that often the most one can hope for is to see a familiar subject from a different angle, or in a different light. Since my own approach when producing books of this nature is to attempt to tell a complete story about a place, sometimes the story line will suggest the idea for a photograph which has not yet been "done." Nonetheless, I am cognizant of the debt I owe to a great many fine photographers who have preceded me to all parts of the islands, and whose work has very often been a guide and inspiration to my own.

I think it is also fair to say that there are very few, if any, photographs in this book (the aquatic shots perhaps aside) which any good amateur photographer could not make; the technology of modern cameras, lenses, and film is such that almost anyone with an "eye" for interesting photographs can produce them. What tends to separate the amateur from the professional photographer today is the commitment the latter makes (and can afford to make) to "getting the shot."

To put that comment in perspective, it may be instructive to know that I spent eleven months, spread out over a year and a half, photographing the islands for this book; in that time I shot nearly 800 rolls of film—about 29,000 frames. (I did not keep a record of the miles I drove, but at one point it was about a thousand miles a week.) Of the 200-odd photographs that appear here, I can think of only a handful which were "grab shots." Only in very rare cases do pictures that "just happen" end up being published. Most published photographs are the result of at least some planning; the stunning shot is more often the end result of a considerable amount of thought, preparation, patience, and persistence. Even then, of course, there are no guarantees: to get my photograph of Kauai's Na Pali coast at sunset, I hiked out to the same vantage point on the Kalalau Trail perhaps 15 times, hoping each time for a spectacular sky. It never came. I am happier with my photograph of the Hanalei Valley, but that shot, too, was the result of perhaps 10 separate visits to the overlook, waiting for just the right combination of late afternoon light and clouds.

I regret that I cannot accommodate the technically-minded with details of exposure, lens used, etc., for I do not keep a record of that information. Like most photographers today, I make heavy use of my through-the-lens light meter, supplemented with both a hand-held incident meter and a spot meter, and still I routinely bracket my exposures. The photographs were made with three different camera systems, using Kodachrome 25 or 64 in all cases. The vast majority of the shots were taken on 35mm film, using Nikon bodies and lenses (from 16mm to 500mm); in some situations, especially detailed scenics where I wanted a higher resolution, I used a Pentax 645 or Pentax 6x7 system, and Kodachrome Professional 120 film.

2. Selected reading: A casual glance through any bookstore in Hawaii will reveal a mountain of books on every imaginable aspect of Hawaii and its history and culture. While the following list is by no means exhaustive, I found the following particularly valuable:

Atlas of Hawaii, by the Department of Geography, University of Hawaii; a wealth of information, statistical and otherwise.

Grapes of Canaan: Hawaii 1820, by Albertine Loomis; a "documentary novel" about Hawaii's earliest missionaries.

Hawaii, by James A. Michener; while Michener's epic novel is not (and does not purport to be) exact history, it is superb at bringing to life certain aspects of Hawaii's past.

Hawaii, A Guide to the Islands, by the Editors, Sunset Books; an excellent guidebook and overall view, particularly useful when touring.

Hawaii: an Uncommon History, by Edward Joesting; selected events of Hawaii's past.

Hawaiian Dictionary, by Mary K. Pukui and Samuel H. Elbert.

The Hawaiian Kingdom (three volumes), by Ralph S. Kuykendall; *the* starting point for a serious study of Hawaiian history from Western "contact" up to 1893; remarkably readable as well.

Hawaii's Best Hiking Trails, by Robert Smith.

Insight Guides, Hawaii, by Apa Productions; another excellent guidebook, particularly thorough on historical and cultural aspects of Hawaii.

Place Names of Hawaii, by Mary K. Pukui, et al.; the standard work on the meaning and origin of Hawaii's place names.

Shoal of Time, a History of the Hawaiian Islands, by Gavan Daws; the best modern overall history.

3. Additional credits: Despite the time I spent in the islands, I was unable to get certain shots which I felt essential to this book, and I am indebted to the following photographers for the photographs cited: Bern Pedit: pages 12-13; Peter French: page 18; Warren Bolster: pages 80-81; Ed Robinson: page 197.

4. Hawaiian words: This is a book in English, and in general English renderings have been used in this book for Hawaiian words, including place names. A full presentation of Hawaiian rendering is outside the scope of this book, but I have deviated from the English rendering in a few places, such as the chapter headings, to give a flavor for the Hawaiian language. For the reader interested in complete Hawaiian rendering (which includes the *okina* and macron) I recommend the appropriate reference works mentioned in *Selected reading* above, or (for place names alone) the superb map series published by the University of Hawaii Press.

Four-year-old Kele Miranda is the darling of a Honolulu hula show.

A Note on the Hawaiian Language

—by Samuel H. Elbert
Emeritus Professor of Pacific Languages
and Linguistics, University of Hawaii

In the distant past, perhaps as early as 500 A.D., the ancestors of today's Hawaiians discovered their future home on a long and perilous canoe trip, perhaps from the Marquesas Islands, some 2200 miles (3500 kilometers) south southeastward of the Hawaiian Islands. The discoverers found eight uninhabited islands with towering peaks, thick forests, coral reefs, snow, and volcanic fires, but perhaps no food except for fish in the sea and the coconuts, breadfruit, taro and bananas they brought with them.

The voyagers brought with them as well a language rich in imagery and symbolism which was central to their lives. An ancient saying illustrates the value the early Hawaiians placed on language:

> *I ka 'ōlelo nō, ke ola,*
> *I ka 'ōlelo nō, ka make.**

> *In language indeed, is life,*
> *In language indeed, is death.**

Remote as it is, Hawai'i is the most distant outpost of the Austronesian language family that extends from Madagascar in the west, to New Zealand in the south, Easter Island in the east, and Hawai'i in the northeast. The language which evolved in these islands was a branch of what linguists today call Proto East Polynesian, consisting of one of the smallest sound systems in the world: just five vowels (long and short), and 10 consonants, eventually simplified to the eight recognized today: h, k, l, m, n, p, w, and the "glottal stop," a sound break as in the English expression "oh-oh," indicated in the written language with the reversed apostrophe (*'okina*).

Grammatically speaking, Hawaiian is both simpler and more complex than some European languages: simpler in that it lacks both declensions and conjugations (although the missionaries chose to see them); more complex in that Hawaiians made subtle distinctions where they are lacking in English, for example. Thus Hawaiian uses different terms for "we" meaning "the two of us" (*kāua*),versus "we" meaning "three or more of us" (*kākou*); other examples abound.

Whatever its degree of simplicity or complexity, Hawaiian endured and evolved for centuries, but wholly as an oral (unwritten) language. With the arrival of Europeans, and especially the New England missionaries, in the early 1820s, things became much more complex. For if the missionary purpose of educating and converting the natives was to proceed, a writing system for Hawaiian was essential. Although they were competent in Greek, Latin, and Hebrew, the missionaries were not trained in modern linguistics, and the writing system they devised ignored both the glottal stop and the distinction between long and short vowels (today indicated by the *macron*, a horizontal line over the vowel, indicating that it is long).

It must of course be remembered that the missionaries were devising a writing system for the purpose of *making literate*, in the English alphabet, *Hawaiians in their native tongue*. The emphasis was on simplicity for rapidity and ease of learning; Hawaiians knew how to pronounce their own language, and could "mentally supply" missing elements such as the 'okina and macron. (It is not, of course, unusual for a writing system to leave much to the knowledge of the speaker: consider the pronunciation of "ou" in the English words though, through, ought, and out.) In a further simplification, the consonants b, d, r, t, and v—included by the missionaries in their original primers—were dropped when it was realized that the Hawaiians replaced them with their own sounds in ordinary conversation. For all its faults, the writing system devised by the reverend grammarians accomplished its purpose, for the Hawaiians achieved literacy with astonishing rapidity.

However, for the purpose of instructing *the non-Hawaiian-speaker in the pronunciation and meaning of Hawaiian*, the writing system devised by the missionaries had severe limitations, especially since—given the very limited sound system—the pronunciation of a word is crucial to its meaning. Take, for example, three words written simply as "ai" by the missionaries. When macron and glottal stop are included, three very different words emerge: *'ai*, 'to eat'; *ai*, 'to make love'; and *'ā'ī*, 'neck.' The name of the island of Lāna'i is another case in point. The meaning of the island's name is often given, erroneously, as "hump" or "swelling." While this is indeed a meaning of "lānai," the correct rendering of the name of the island is "Lāna'i"—a completely different word with an entirely different pronunciation. A possible meaning for the island's correct name is "day of conquest."

Later linguists, with a wider purpose in mind, have stressed the importance of the macron and 'okina, and over time they have become integral parts of the Hawaiian spelling system, increasingly shown on street signs and in other writings. With these additions, Hawaiian is fairly easy for non-speakers to pronounce, thus, "a" as in father; "e" as in egg; "i" as in marine; "o" as in over; and "u" as in rule.

The question of the meaning of the names of the other Hawaiian Islands often arises: Hawai'i itself has no meaning in Hawaiian, but in other parts of Polynesia is the name given the ancestral homeland. Maui was derived from the demigod Māui, common in many Pacific cultures. The remaining island names, despite claims in much casual literature, have no generally accepted meanings, although there is some evidence that Kaho'olawe means "taking away," with reference to the action of ocean currents.

But no technical discussion of the language should be allowed to obscure the essential point that language to the Hawaiians was a matter of life and of death, and was at the same time the means of celebrating the beauty of the islands in thousands of chants and songs. One of the most moving was composed in the early 1920s by Henry Waia'u. Based on an old Kaua'i legend, it reveals in poetic language the Hawaiians' appreciation for some of the manifestations of nature, with scarcely veiled implications of love:

> *Ma'ema'e wale ke kino o ka palai*
> *Pulupē i ka ua li'ili'i kilikilihune*
> *A he wehi ia no ka uka o ka nahele*
> *He moani ke 'ala i lawe 'ia mai,*
> *Hu'ihu'i, konikoni ē*

> Clean is the body of the fern
> Wet in the fine and gentle rain
> That is the adornment of forest uplands
> And the bearer of sweet perfumes,
> Coolness, and palpitations **

* *Proverb 1191 in* Nā 'Ōlelo No'eau, *by Mary Kawena Pukui, Bishop Museum Press; reprinted with permission.*
** *From* Nā mele o Hawai'i nei, 101 Hawaiian Songs, *by Samuel H. Elbert and Noelani Mahoe, University of Hawaii Press; reprinted with permission.*

Acknowledgments

Having been a reader far longer than a writer, I know that this is a section usually given little notice by most readers. It should not be so, at least with a book of this nature, for it owes a great deal to the generous cooperation of an untold number of people. I am particularly indebted to Watters O. Martin, Jr. of Honolulu, and Father Fernandez of Kalaupapa, for reading and commenting on portions of the text; it should go without saying that responsibility for its content is entirely my own. The contribution of many other individuals and institutions will be apparent from the text or from the credits at the photographs themselves, and I would like to express my gratitude to them, and also to:

Sheraton Hotels; Marguerite Rho, Alexander & Baldwin; Castle & Cooke; Hawaii Visitors Bureau;
on Kauai:
Bob Stuhr and Murrayair; Bill Enoka; John Herkes, McBryde Sugar Co.;
Westin Kauai; Kauai Museum; Grove Farm Plantation; Hanalei
Elementary School;
on Oahu:
Mission Children's Society; Betty Kam, Roger Rose, Bishop Museum;
Don Severson; Kamehameha Schools/Bishop Estate; Oahu Sugar Co.;
Kamaha Hawaii; Randy Sanborn and the Manu O Ke Kai Canoe Club;
Watters O. Martin, Jr.; Rev. Egen Yoshikami; United States Army; United
States Navy; Admiral Diego Hernandez; Mike Hassett and Avant-Aire;
Punahou School; Halekulani Hotel; The Friends of Iolani Palace; Wright
Bowman, Jr.; Ray Sakuma Productions; State Foundation on Culture
and the Arts; Daughters of Hawaii; Kaahumanu Society; Leslie K.
Nunes; Del Monte Corporation; Campbell Estate; Ala Moana Hotel; Ray
Wong; Michael Garcia;
on Molokai and Lanai:
Dole Company (Castle & Cooke); Roger Art; Father Fernandez; Nature
Conservancy; Molokai Ranch; Kumu Hula Moana Dudoit and halau;
George Maioho; John Lichnowsky;
on Maui:
Jack Dixon; Lahaina Restoration Foundation; Lahainaluna School;
Lahaina Scrimshaw; Lahaina Printsellers; Hawaiian Commercial &
Sugar Co.; Auntie Emma Sharpe; Arleone Dibben-Young; Pacific Whale
Foundation; Ed Rice, Ulupalakua Ranch; Haleakala Ranch; Bradish
Johnson, Protea Gardens of Maui;
on Hawaii:
Institute for Astronomy, University of Hawaii; Tom Peek, Bob McLaren,
Tony Sylvester, Ron Kohler, David Beattie, Ian McLean, Malcom Smith
(Mauna Kea observatories); Kawaihae Canoe Club; Hawaii Volcano
Observatory; Scott Lopez, Hawaii Volcanoes National Park; Ken
Dillingham; Hilo Coast Processors; Hamakua Sugar Co.; Dan Hata; Puna
Orchids, Inc.; Hilo Hawaiian Hotel; King Kamehameha Hotel; Lyman
Museum; Aaron Hegerfeldt;
and in California:
Marie LaBrucherie, Ella LaBrucherie, and Martha Hoch.

Index

Hawaii

Location, geography and climate: *Hawaii is an island chain or archipelago of volcanic origin composed of 132 islands containing 6471 square miles (16,641 square kilometers; in area Hawaii is 47th among the 50 States) and extending over some 1600 miles (2500 kilometers) on a northwest-southeast axis. Eight of the islands are regarded as "major" (listed below), while the remaining 124 tiny islets, most of which are found north and west of Kauai, have a total area of barely three square miles. The major islands lie in the north central Pacific, just south of the Tropic of Cancer, and are one of the most isolated island groups in the world. Honolulu is 2400 miles south and west of San Francisco, the nearest point on the Mainland. The latitude of the major islands is approximately that of Mexico City and Hong Kong. Prevailing trade winds from the northeast create generally rainy windward slopes and drier leeward sides; the near-constant breezes and surrounding ocean result in a mild, subtropical year-round climate.*

Government: *50th State of the United States (admitted 1959); tripartite government (executive, legislative and judicial branches) under a state constitution.*

Economy: *Based principally on tourism, military and civilian government installations, sugar, pineapple, and diversified agriculture.*

Miscellaneous: *State Motto—Ua mau ke ea o ka aina i ka pono (The life of the land is preserved in righteousness); Bird—nene; Flower—hibiscus; Tree—Kukui.*

Population: 1,062,000 (all population figures are 1986 estimates); density—164 per square mile.

Niihau: area—73 sq. miles; highest elevation—1281 ft.; population—250.

Kauai: area—553 sq. miles; highest elevation—5243 ft.; population—46,300.

Oahu: area—608 sq. miles; highest elevation—4,020 ft; population—816,700.

Molokai: area—260 sq. miles; highest elevation—4,970 ft.; population—6,700.

Lanai: area—141 sq. miles; highest elevation—3,370 ft.; population—2,200.

Maui: area—728 sq. miles; highest elevation—10,023 ft.; population—78,600.

Kahoolawe: area—45 sq. miles; highest elevation—1477 ft.; unpopulated.

Hawaii (Big Island): area—4,037 sq. miles; highest elevation—13,796 ft.; population—111,800.

Site of a cattle and sheep ranch, Niihau is under the sole ownership of a single family, and open to outsiders by invitation only. Home to a mere 250 inhabitants—nearly all Native Hawaiians—the island remains a unique preserve where Hawaiian is spoken on a daily basis.

KAUAI

NIIHAU

Hanalei

Kapaa

Waialeale 5148

Waimea

Koloa

Lihue

Kauai Channel

Oahu's population and economic dominance of the islands began shortly after the arrival of the first Westerners: Honolulu Harbor provided the only adequate anchorage for European-style ships. The the transfer of the capital there from Lahaina, the eventual development of Pearl Harbor as a military base, and the growth of trade from abroad assured Honolulu's preeminent position. Today Oahu contains over three quarters of the State's population.

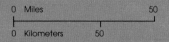

0   Miles   50

0   Kilometers   50

161° W   160° W   159° W

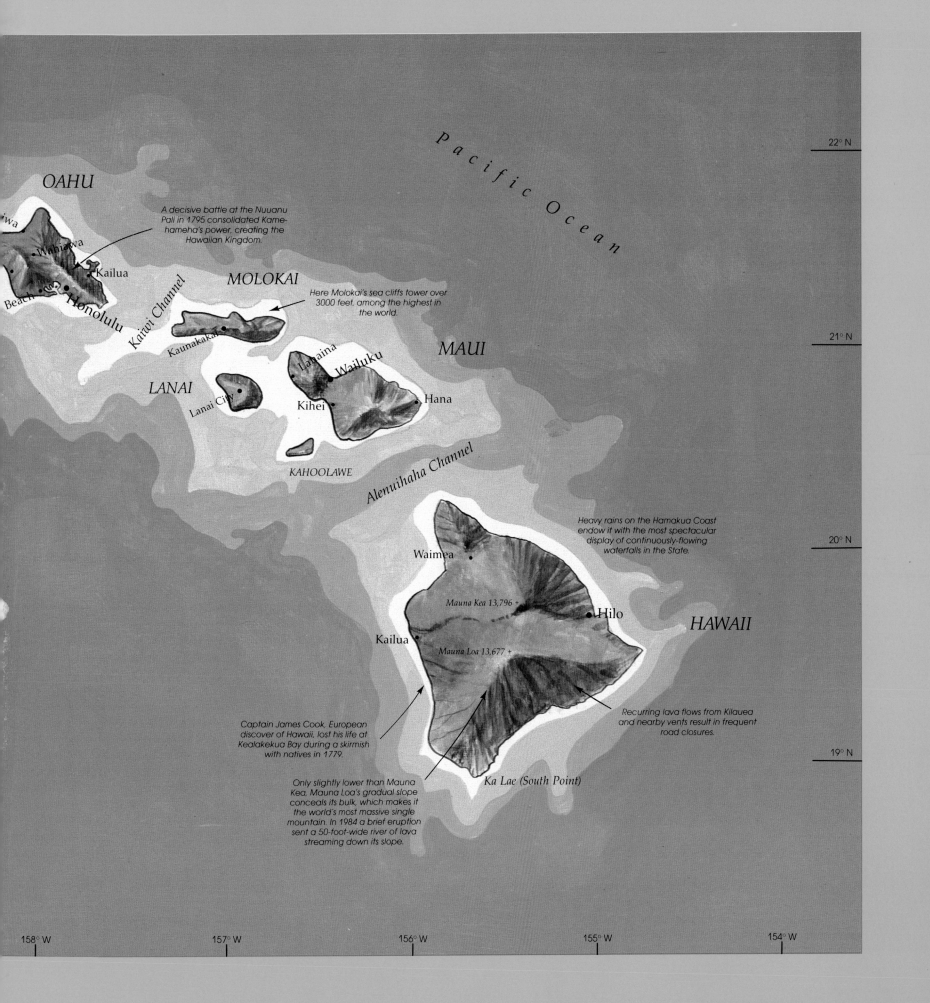

22° N

OAHU

A decisive battle at the Nuuanu Pali in 1795 consolidated Kamehameha's power, creating the Hawaiian Kingdom.

iwa

Wahiawa

Kailua

Beach

Honolulu

Kaiwi Channel

MOLOKAI

Here Molokai's sea cliffs tower over 3000 feet, among the highest in the world.

Kaunakakai

21° N

LANAI

Lanai City

Lahaina

Wailuku

MAUI

Kihei

Hana

KAHOOLAWE

Alenuihaha Channel

Heavy rains on the Hamakua Coast endow it with the most spectacular display of continuously-flowing waterfalls in the State.

Waimea

20° N

Mauna Kea 13,796 +

Hilo

HAWAII

Kailua

Mauna Loa 13,677 +

Recurring lava flows from Kilauea and nearby vents result in frequent road closures.

Captain James Cook, European discover of Hawaii, lost his life at Kealakekua Bay during a skirmish with natives in 1779.

19° N

Only slightly lower than Mauna Kea, Mauna Loa's gradual slope conceals its bulk, which makes it the world's most massive single mountain. In 1984 a brief eruption sent a 50-foot-wide river of lava streaming down its slope.

Ka Lae (South Point)

158° W   157° W   156° W   155° W   154° W

Author-photographer Roger LaBrucherie received his education at Harvard College and Stanford University, taking degrees in law and economics from the latter. Prior to Hawaiian World, Hawaiian Heart *he produced five books in the Caribbean area, including books on Puerto Rico, Barbados, Bermuda, and the Dominican Republic. He makes his home in his native California.*

Design consultant: Martha Hoch

Map paintings by Patrick Waters, El Centro, California

Imagenes Press
P. O. Box 1080
Pine Valley, California 92062 USA
Tel: (619) 352-2188 / 488-3184

Printed and bound in Hong Kong by Everbest Printing Co., Ltd.

Hawaiian World, Hawaiian Heart
ISBN 0-939302-15-2 (Trade Edition) / ISBN 0-939302-16-0 (Deluxe Edition)

Also available in a Japanese-language edition.

10 9 8 7 6 5 4 3 2 1